REDEMPTIVE HISTORY
AND THE
NEW TESTAMENT SCRIPTURES

Formerly
THE AUTHORITY
OF THE
NEW TESTAMENT SCRIPTURES

By
HERMAN RIDDERBOS

Translated by
H. De Jongste

Revised by
Richard B. Gaffin, Jr.

Presbyterian and Reformed Publishing Company
Phillipsburg, New Jersey

Translated from the Dutch edition *Heilsgeschiedenis en Heilige Schrift van het Nieuwe Testament. Het Gezag van het Nieuwe Testament* (Kampen: J.H. Kok N.V., 1955).

Manufactured in the United States of America.

Library of Congress Cataloging-in-Publication Data

Ridderbos, Herman N.
  Redemptive history and the New Testament Scriptures.

  Translation of: Heilsgeschiedenis en heilige schrift van het Nieuwe Testament.
  Bibliography: p.
  Includes index.
  1. Bible. N.T.—Evidences, authority, etc.
2. Bible. N.T.—Inspiration. 3. Bible. N.T.—Canon.
4. Reformed Church—Doctrines. I. Gaffin, Richard B.
II. Title.
BS2332.R5313 1988   225   87-32875
ISBN 0-87552-416-8

CONTENTS

ABBREVIATIONS

ET   English Translation

EvT   *Evangelische Theologie*

GThT   *Gereformeerd Theologisch Tijdschrift*

NedTT   *Nederlands Theologisch Tijdschrift*

RE   *Realencyklopädie für protestantische Theologie und Kirche*

RGG   *Religion in Geschichte und Gegenwart*

ST   *Studia Theologica*

Str-B   H. Strack and P. Billerbeck, *Kommentar zum Neuen Testament*

TBl   *Theologische Blätter*

TDNT   G. Kittel and G. Friedrich, *Theological Dictionary of the New Testament*

TLZ   *Theologische Literaturzeitung*

TR   *Theologische Rundschau*

TZ   *Theologische Zeitschrift*

ZTK   *Zeitschrift für Theologie und Kirche*

FOREWORD TO THE REVISED TRANSLATION

The original translation has been carefully reviewed, corrected, and smoothed out in numerous places. Citations in foreign languages other than Dutch have been translated or, where possible, cited from existing English translations. Bibliographical references have been standardized.

Special thanks to John J. Hughes of Whitefish, Montana, for many hours spent in making countless suggestions to improve the readability of the translation, as well as for preparing the manuscript for publication. His help has been invaluable. My thanks also to the Board of Trustees of Westminster Theological Seminary, Pennsylvania, for a leave of absence during the first semester and winter term of 1985–1986, in part to complete this project, and to the publishers for their commitment to make this valuable, still timely work available once more to English-speaking readers.

Richard B. Gaffin, Jr.
October 1987

1. Introduction

Any scientific investigation of Scripture repeatedly confronts the issue of the character of the Bible's authority. Most contemporary biblical scholars believe that no special divine authority can be ascribed to Scripture as such and that its authority can be spoken of only in connection with its content. Proponents of that position do not deny all revelation or every form of special revelation; instead they distinguish in principle between revelation and Scripture. According to them, the Scripture is only the human record of divine revelation or a human witness to revelation. Scripture as such does not have any revelatory quality, and so in spite of the sublime nature of the subject matter, biblical writings are thought to be no different from ordinary human literature. Therefore the Bible is to be investigated and judged by the same standards that we apply to all other human documents.[1]

Of course, the question of the nature of Scripture's authority cannot be answered so simply, for we are still faced with the problem of biblical criticism.[2] If Scripture is not itself divine revelation, if it is simply a faulty, human medium, then what standards shall we use to establish the authority of its content? Must that be left to the faith of those who read the Bible? Does science have anything to say? Or must a person abandon himself to the voice of the Spirit, who makes the fallible human word His instrument? In the midst of such divergent views about its revelatory content, is it still possible to appeal to Scripture as an authority? Can we continue to base doctrine on the Bible? What is the significance of the expression "obedience to Scripture?" Is there any principial reason to distinguish as canonical the Bible's writings from other human documents?[3]

Although such questions can easily be multiplied, one thing is clear: the problem of biblical criticism, no matter how illuminating, does not legitimate faith in Scripture. Certainty cannot result from uncertainty, nor can biblical criticism pronounce Scripture to be authoritative. Rather, the tenuous character of biblical criticism once more raises the question of the basis and nature of the Bible's authority. Involved here are not only matters for scientific discussion; no less at stake is the tie that binds churches in the Reformation tradition to their heritage—the unequivocal confession of the revelatory character and authority of Scripture. The Belgic Confession (Article 5), for example, after listing the canonical writings, states:

> We receive all these books, and these only, as holy and canonical, for the regulation, foundation, and confirmation of our faith; believing without any doubt all things contained in them, not so much because the church receives and approves them as such, but more especially because the Holy Spirit witnesses in our hearts that they are from God.

Those who believe that such a personally expressed confession is not a dead letter will insist that the scientific study of the Bible may not evade the force of those words. Human life is a unity. Both the head and the heart are involved in our faith as well as in our scientific study of the Bible. To confess Scripture as canonical and authoritative raises special questions for the biblical scholar. It is not that such a confession becomes less of a joy and more of a burden to the degree that one approaches Scripture scientifically or more of a joy and less of a burden to the extent that one approaches the Bible as a simple believer. The allegedly simple believer's faith in Scripture is confronted with questions, conflicts, and temptations that are just as difficult as any encountered by his presumably more sophisticated counterpart. Theology, like every other scientific endeavor, is an expression of life—life that struggles for deliverance and only triumphs in God's light. For that reason, there is a close connection between the church and theology. On the one hand, the church confronts biblical scholars with its confession and follows their scientific investigation of Scripture with great interest. The church's motivation is not the mistaken and conceited idea that it is the guardian of science but an awareness that its own interests are at stake. On the other hand, its relation to the church, the living people of God, should impart to theology a deep awareness of the nature of its own object.

The manner in which the scientific investigation of Scripture proceeds brings its own joy and problems. Biblical scholars have tools and techniques at their disposal that in many respects facilitate a clearer understanding of Scripture. They are also better equipped to discern the questions raised by its character as Scripture. They investigate the historical background of the different books of the Bible and seek to learn how the various writings were brought together into a single canon. In that investigation they encounter analogies and similarities with other writings and with other religious concepts and practices. They discover the different literary forms and varying content of the Bible—a diversity that often appears to be a function of Scripture's humanity. Thus biblical scholars are confronted with the necessity of attempting to formulate the relationship between revelation and Scripture, between the Bible as the Word of God and the Bible as the word of man.

Traditionally, theologians who have acknowledged Scripture's authority in terms of the church's confession cited above have determined that relationship by appealing to the so-called self-attestation, or self-witness, of Scripture. The manner in which the New Testament speaks of the Old is especially important. Since the New Testament canon is not followed by a subsequent canonical addition, there is no such general witness to it. Nevertheless, besides the analogy with the Old Testament, the self-attestation of the individual New Testament writings yields considerable relevant data.[4] These formal pronouncements of Scripture's authority, however, are valid only to those who already accept the authority of the Bible. Logically speaking, that is a form of circular reasoning. Certainly, *every* appeal to Scripture is ultimately based on its binding authority for faith,[5] no matter how exactly that authority is understood. Nevertheless, just those who confess that the Scriptures "are of God" feel the need for further reflection on their revelatory character. Obviously, the Bible is not a heavenly gift that arrived all at once as a finished divine, revelatory entity. Scripture has a history. It is a product of God's revelatory activity in the history of redemption. Therefore the revelatory character of the Bible should not be separated in a mechanical fashion from the history of redemption in which it came into being, for its revelatory character is neither an isolated phenomenon nor derived only from formal statements of Scripture concerning its authority. Thus the significance of the Bible and the nature of its authority can properly be understood only by closely relating Scripture to the history of redemption. Again we must reason in a circle since the history of redemption is known solely from Scripture. Thus in this study we are not seeking an extrabiblical basis for faith. Rather, we are seeking to delineate the essence of Scripture and the nature of its authority within the framework of the history of redemption; we are seeking to clarify *the relationship between the history of redemption and Scripture.*

For reasons that will become clear, I shall limit the investigation to the *New Testament* Scriptures. First I will investigate the New Testament canon and then the nature of its authority in the light of New Testament redemptive history, that is, in the light of the coming and work of Jesus

Christ in the fullness of time. In doing so, it is not my purpose to formulate a complete doctrine of Scripture but to offer an exegetical, redemptive-historical contribution to that doctrine.

CHAPTER I

THE CANON OF THE NEW TESTAMENT

A. QUESTIONS OF PRINCIPLE

2. Recent Reflections

Any discussion of principial issues about the New Testament canon and its acceptance by the Christian church[1] must begin by recognizing that current Protestant literature on this topic is scanty and unclear.[2] Strathmann, a Lutheran exegete who wrote about the crisis of the canon, called the unclear relationship between the church and the canon a "creeping sickness" suffered by modern Protestant Christianity.[3] Others, like Kümmel, have added their approval to that type of criticism. According to Kümmel, Christians generally accept the canon without clearly understanding the necessity for a fixed set of early Christian writings and with no concern about the correctness of the present collection.[4]

Such uncertainty is a result of the strong influence of post-Enlightenment biblical criticism on theology and so in the life of the church. The impetus for applying rationalistic criticism to the study of the New Testament canon came from Johann Salomo Semler's four-volume work, *Abhandlung von freier Untersuchung des Kanons* (1771–1775). On the basis of his historical investigations, Semler challenged the beliefs that from the beginning the church had accepted the canon with great unanimity and that the canon bears the marks of divinity. Semler focused attention on the uncertainty, conflict, human strategy, and ecclesiastical policy and tactics that eventually led to the formation of the twenty-seven-book canon as an untouchable ecclesiastical entity. He asked how good Protestants who did not believe in the infallibility of the church could question anyone's right to criticize the church's position on the canon. He argued that the history of the canon is in conflict with the authority ascribed to it and that those who assembled the books of the New Testament never intended to establish an absolute, unbreakable norm for faith, thought, and action. According to Semler, the canon was understood simply as the list of books that might be read in public worship, the books that the bishops thought were the most suitable and in the best interests of good order. What individual church members could read did not fall under that regula-

1

tion. Thus Semler argued that the canon was a matter of ecclesiastical discipline, not personal faith. Semler believed that by its very nature, personal faith is not subject to any external and binding authority because it is grounded inwardly in true religious and moral knowledge. He argued that if it is proper to speak of the witness of the Holy Spirit, that witness has nothing to do with authenticating a certain number of books, much less with their selection. The witness of the Spirit is related solely to religious and moral knowledge, insofar as such knowledge finds expression in the New Testament books.[5]

In the final analysis, Semler's criticism heralded a complete abandonment of Scripture as a canon, as a divine norm for faith and life. Nevertheless, his historical perspectives greatly influenced subsequent New Testament studies and have been used repeatedly to call into question the New Testament's authority as a canon. All secular historical approaches to the authority of the New Testament deny its normative status as canon for the church and theology, and they do so in an a priori fashion, as the great historical-critical schools of the last century demonstrated. Accordingly, as time passed, many scholars flatly rejected the church's enduring belief in the authority of the New Testament.[6] They believed that historical scholarship was the best way to judge the canonicity of the New Testament. F. Chr. Baur, for example, said that the main task of New Testament Introduction is the critical investigation of the principle of the canonical authority of the New Testament documents.[7] Such an approach clearly resulted in the abandonment of the idea of canon and the subjection of the church's faith to historical scholarship.

Other scholars saw the absurdity of that result. They believed that their historical investigation should (and could!) detach itself from every a priori of faith. They sought to resolve the difficulty by strictly separating what they called the historical and the dogmatic approaches to the New Testament. To canonics (scientific introduction) they ascribed an exclusively historical significance. According to Jülicher-Fascher, canonics limits itself to the twenty-seven books simply because of their acquired historic significance, which has given them the status of a unique historical entity.[8] The task of New Testament Introduction, therefore, consists neither in the defense of the divine character of these writings nor in their criticism.[9] New Testament Introduction is concerned solely with a critical description of the origin of the canon. Questions concerning a priori views that have been or might be held about the origin and collection of these writings should be left entirely to the study of the history of dogma and to

2

dogmatic theology. New Testament Introduction itself has nothing at all to do with such questions.

This method, which has been followed in most recent Introductions to the New Testament, is preferable to the method of Baur and his school because its descriptive approach seeks to avoid passing judgment on what is and what is not canonical and authoritative for the church. Clearly, however, separating the theological and historical perspectives can neither cure the creeping sickness suffered by the church because of uncertainty about its foundation nor remedy the situation that divorces the study of the canon from Christian faith, thereby completely robbing such study of its theological character. Therefore it is not surprising that New Testament scholars have been dissatisfied with this dichotomy and have sought to unite the historical study of the formation of the canon with a theological appraisal of its significance. That the canon was formed after a long ecclesiastical development is not necessarily incompatible with the special authority that the church has ascribed to it. The most important question in that regard is simply this: "What is the basis for the church's recognition both of the canon as such and of the twenty-seven books in particular, and what light does careful investigation of the history of the canon shed on this recognition of the canon as Holy Scripture?"

3. Appeals to Luther's Standpoint

Appeal to Luther's view of the canon has played a significant role in recent historical criticism of the New Testament. With the other Reformers, Luther opposed the Roman Catholic doctrine of tradition by forcefully proclaiming that Scripture is the only accessible source of special revelation. Nevertheless, Luther was sharply critical of various New Testament books. His criticism was not limited to James (which in the preface to his 1522 edition of the New Testament he compared to the main books of the New Testament as "really an epistle of straw, for it has nothing of the nature of the gospel in it"), but extended as well to Jude, Hebrews, and Revelation, though later he changed his mind about some of those writings.[10]

Luther's critique was not primarily motivated by historical-critical considerations but by material concerns. In his judgment, the questionable books did not speak of Christ in the manner of the "right, certain chief books of the New Testament," especially in the manner of the main Pauline Epistles. "What preaches and urges Christ" was for Luther the criterion of apostolicity and canonicity. Undoubtedly, he did not intend to make the content of revelation subjective; rather he sought to emphasize as forcefully as possible what he regarded as the central message of the gospel. Defining canonicity in terms of "what urges Christ," however, introduced the principle of *a canon within the canon*. This principle not only focuses attention on the heart of the gospel but also has a critical, discriminating significance.

Orthodox Lutherans later rejected this standpoint and affirmed the canonicity of the twenty-seven books of the New Testament without reservation, but many people, especially in reaction to the skepticism of the Enlightenment, appealed (and continue to appeal) to Luther. Such appeal, on the one hand, is made to justify historical or theological criticism of the canon, and on the other hand to support the canon as the only rule and guide of the church. The great Lutheran exegete Th. Zahn, for example, wrote in an infrequently cited but rich monograph on the abiding significance of the New Testament canon[11] that the reserve with which the Lutheran confessions speak of the biblical canon ought not to be regarded as a deficiency but as a blessing, as "a gracious protection of God."[12]

The Lutheran confessions do not list the canonical writings of the Old and New Testaments, as many Reformed confessions do. Zahn believed this omission was the result of the influence of Luther's critical attitude, an influence for which we ought to be thankful. He believed that though Luther may not be right in every detail, in principle such a critical acceptance of the New Testament is alone correct, and he appealed to various passages in the New Testament for support, for example where the church is exhorted to "examine everything carefully; hold fast to that which is good" (1 Thess. 5:21) and where the church is told that the spirits of the prophets are subject to criticism (1 Cor. 14:32). According to Zahn, texts like those make it a duty for biblical scholars to investigate even the New Testament critically.[13] Zahn did not believe that the canon was closed and established with finality, and he was sharply critical of Reformed scholars[14] who, with their doctrines of inspiration and of the internal testimony of the Holy Spirit, would silence every criticism in an a priori fashion. In opposition to the Reformed viewpoint, Zahn argued that the message of the gospel is determinative of the canon and is the basis, firmly established by faith, on which the church must judge which writings are canonical. Only then can the church effectively withstand criticism that is alien to its faith. Criticism is not defeated simply by forbidding every form of criticism; it is only defeated by scientific criticism that is rooted in the

4

faith of the church, by criticism that confirms, rather than destroys, the true dimensions of the New Testament.[15]

Zahn emphasized the historical development and ecclesiastical character of the canon and the necessity to combat historical criticism with its own weapons. He also attempted to combine Luther's concept of the canon with a subjectively tinged theology: the canon is the canon and Scripture is the Word of God only insofar as that is the church's understanding. This argument, with the idea of canon completely attuned to the perception of faith, is the one used in most contemporary circles to maintain belief in the canon and at the same time to allow for the historical-critical investigation of its content and extent. In fact, this view means that in its concrete form, the canon as a normative principle for the church now functions in a material, not a formal, sense. To support this position, people like to appeal to Luther's statement that the canon is "what urges Christ." But in modern biblical scholarship, this principle is applied far more critically than it was by Luther and involves an increasingly far-reaching emphasis on faith, whether of the church or of the individual, for determining what may still be received as canon in the material sense.

Strathmann, for example, writes that this modern development of Luther's principle allows one to make a "completely unprejudiced appraisal" of the New Testament writings from religious and historical perspectives and that this insures the impossibility of misusing Scripture in a doctrinaire or juridical fashion.[16] H. Faber also appeals to Luther for justification of his liberal view of the canon.[17] In his study of the necessity and limits of the New Testament canon, Kümmel likewise appeals to Luther[18] on the decisive point in question. In fact, Kümmel believes that Luther's critical principle should be extended to the entire content of the canon. According to Kümmel, it makes no sense to continue the sixteenth-century discussion about which books belong in the canon. Instead we should apply Luther's critical principle to the whole canon, that is, we should discern where in the canon witness to Jesus Christ elicits faith.[19] In practice we have to deal with the existing canon for it belongs to the entire church, and changing it would be difficult. But that does not mean that the decisions of the ancient church must bind us. The New Testament writings are canonical only to the extent that each of them measures up to the norm for our faith,[20] that is, brings us into a relationship with the historical revelation of Jesus Christ and its significance for faith.[21] The latter is found, according to Kümmel, in the "central proclamation" of the New Testament, a proclamation that must be established by a critical comparison of its various writings. For Kümmel, the canon is a necessity because the historical character of God's definitive revelation in Christ cannot be experienced apart from the New Testament writings. The boundaries of the canon run through the middle of the New Testament and can be defined only by constantly reflecting on its central proclamation of Christ and by studying the entire New Testament and the noncanonical literature of the early church.[22]

Other scholars (with a similar understanding of the canon) deny this concept of an *objective canon within the canon*. They define the canonicity of the New Testament in terms of repeatedly encountering *the Word of God* in it *as a contemporary event*. For example, Diem writes that the final basis for Scripture's canonicity is that it "permits itself to be preached,"[23] that is, the church has heard the Word of God in the event of preaching.[24] For Diem, the present concrete form of the biblical canon cannot be justified in principle but only de facto, that is, by experiencing the self-evidencing nature of Scripture in the context of its proclamation.[25] That does not mean, however, where Scripture cannot be preached or where a person encounters open contradictions in it (the existence of which is not to be denied) that the canon may or must be narrowed or that a perpetually valid canon within the canon can be established. The canon must be acknowledged as the place where the church universal has heard the Word of God. Through the canon Christ speaks the word that we need for each situation. His freedom to do so, even through its theological contradictions, must remain unimpaired.[26] Consequently, Diem seeks the canonicity of Scripture in the fact that many have heard and continue to hear Christ in the event of preaching. Thus he replaces the ideas of a fixed historical canon and of a canon within a canon with the idea of the present-day self-witness of Christ in the Scriptures.

The radical extent to which this principle can be carried is evident in Käsemann's position.[27] According to Käsemann, the New Testament is full of contradictions. Rather than providing a foundation for the unity of the church, the New Testament constitutes a basis for the diversity of ecclesiastical confessions.[28] If binding authority were ascribed to the canon in its entirety, each different ecclesiastical confession could appeal to it with more or less equal validity. But where one appeals in principle to "it is written," critical scholarship cannot escape the truth of Lessing's story of the three rings in *Nathan the Wise*. Anyone who believes that Scripture in its objectivity is a divine authority abstracts it from the Spirit, who "in an always new and contemporaneous way" will guide us into all truth (John 16:13). In its "naked objectivity" the canon is neither the Word of

God nor is it identical with the gospel. It is the Word of God only insofar as it is and repeatedly becomes the gospel. The question "What is the gospel?" cannot be answered by the historian; it can only be answered by the believer who has been convinced by the Spirit and who has ears to hear. The gospel is not known by the *beati possidentes* ("blessed possessors"); it is recognized by the uncertain and the tempted, in and despite the confessions, with and even in opposition to the New Testament canon.[29]

The problems raised by such views of the canon are readily apparent. Granting that a principle is not always to be judged by its most extreme consequences, it is nevertheless undeniable that new problems arise whenever the Scriptures are no longer regarded as the exclusive principle of canonicity, when something else is substituted, for example the principle of a canon within the canon or the contemporaneous speaking of God in and through Scripture. This raises the question of how to determine and validate such new principles of canonicity. To what extent can a person use such principles and still speak of the canon as an objective standard and norm? This question is especially relevant for the prevailing view, advanced with such great certainty, that the Word of God in Scripture is a contemporary event and that the New Testament becomes the canon "again and again." This view is undoubtedly a modification of Lutheran theology, which from its inception understood the Word of God to be the gospel as it functions in *preaching*,[30] the *viva vox* of Christ[31] that coincides with the operation of the Holy Spirit through the Word.[32] But no matter how much truth it may contain, this view is beset with danger. By identifying the Word of God exclusively with the Spirit's operation in preaching, this view continuously risks identifying first the Word of God and then the canon with what the church understands. This position may even result in identifying God's Word with what an individual person experiences when the Scriptures are preached; it leaves the door wide open to a subjective and existentialist view of God's Word and of the canon.

The foregoing remarks are not meant to imply that those who hold to a canon within the canon (whether in an objective or subjective, actualistic sense) no longer ascribe any meaning to the canon of Scripture. Many different steps have been taken to uphold the necessity of the biblical canon[33] and to guard against subjectivism and spiritualism.[34] But one fact remains. The final decision as to what the church deems to be holy and unimpeachable does not reside in the biblical canon itself. Human judgment about what is essential and central for Christian faith is the final court of appeal. This judgment may be based on the historical-critical method, on the

7

church's experience of faith, or on the moment of hearing God's Word in preaching. One thing, however, is certain: such theories diminish in principle the significance of *Scripture* as the canon, no matter how broad the spectrum of differences among the various advocates of this viewpoint may be.

4. The Reformed View

From its inception, *Reformed theology* has differed with Luther on the issue of the canon. During the Reformation, Reformed theologians acknowledged the existing canon without reservation. They did not concur with Luther's objections against specific books, and they did not subject the content or the extent of the canon to a new criterion.[35] Unlike the Lutheran confessions, the major Reformed confessions list the canonical books by name. As a result, Reformed theology placed a strong emphasis on the objective significance of the Word of God, in distinction from a subjective acceptance of it. Reformed theologians drew a clear distinction between the canon as such and its recognition by the church.

To the degree that Reformed theology has remained faithful to its starting point, it has continually rejected the Roman Catholic doctrine of the canon, the belief that faith in the canon rests on the authority of the church. But it has been no less vehement in its protest against any subjectivistic or actualistic view that would define the canon either in terms of the experience of faith or in terms of the church's momentary understanding of the Word of God.

Therefore it is not at all surprising that historical critics subsequently attacked this "objective" and clearly defined understanding of canon. The crucial problem for Reformed theology at this point is to explain why it recognizes only the twenty-seven books of the New Testament as canonical. Reformed theologians do not justify the acceptance of the canon by appealing to a "canon within the canon." Nor do they appeal to its recognition by the church or to the experience of faith or to a recurring, actualistic understanding of the Word of God as canon. And so the question naturally arises, "On what basis does Reformed theology accept the canon?"

The Reformed understanding of the canon was sharply attacked by Zahn.[36] He accused Reformed scholars of pretending to have an infallible criterion of canonicity (the witness of the Holy Spirit in their hearts), on the basis of which they believed they could specify in their confessions which books are canonical and which are not. Furthermore, Zahn argued that such an appeal to the witness of the Holy Spirit ignores the uncertainties that have arisen in the history of the canon, appears to make the Holy Spirit the exclusive possession of those who are Reformed, and conflicts with the character of the witness of the Holy Spirit as described in the New Testament. According to Zahn, Calvin's reply to perennial objections about the canonicity of books like James belongs to the most superficial comments ever written on the topic of the canon.[37]

But Zahn's criticism rests on a misconception of the Reformed view of the Word of God in general and of the canon in particular. In opposition to the Roman Catholic doctrine that the authority of the Word of God can only be guaranteed by the church, Calvin appealed not only to the witness of the Holy Spirit in the hearts of believers but above all to the self-attestation of the Scriptures.[38] The divine character of the Bible itself gives it its authority. This divine character is so evident that anyone who has eyes to see is directly convinced and does not need the mediation of the church.[39] The principle of the self-attestation of Scripture as the real ground or source of its recognition as a rule for faith and life is reiterated again and again by subsequent Reformed authors. According to Bavinck, "The canonicity of the books of the Bible is rooted in their existence. They have authority in and of themselves, *iure suo*, simply because they exist."[40] And Karl Barth wrote, "The Bible makes itself to be canon."[41]

Corresponding to this objective principle of the self-attestation of Scripture, from its inception Reformed theology has expressly distinguished the subjective principle of the *testimonium Spiritus Sancti*. The Holy Spirit bears witness to himself not only *through* the Word (in the self-attestation of Scripture as the Word of God) but also *with* the Word, that is, He opens blind eyes to the divine light that shines in the Scriptures. Later Reformed theology has correctly emphasized the fact that the internal witness of the Spirit is not the basis for but the means by which the canon of Scripture is recognized and accepted as the indubitable Word of God.[42] True, after a summary of the canonical books, the Belgic Confession states that we believe all that is included in them without any doubt, not so much "because the church" accepts them and regards them as canonical but in particular "*because* the Holy Spirit" bears witness in our hearts to them that they are from God (Article 5, emphasis added). In view of the place that the entire doctrine of the *testimonium Spiritus Sancti* occupies in older Reformed theology, however, the second "because" should not be understood to mean that the working of the Spirit in the hearts of Christians is the proper basis for the recognition of the divine character of

Scripture. Rather, the proper basis for that is located in Scripture itself, namely in the divine character that emanates from it.[43]

Still, there can be no doubt that though Christians are bound to Scripture by the authority that proceeds from it as God's Word, this does not provide an exact *concept* of its canonicity or of the extent of its authority. The self-attestation of Scripture as understood by Christians through the witness of the Holy Spirit is related above all to the divine character of the central content of Scripture. Scripture's self-attestation does not provide direct and infallible certainty about all the facts and data in the New Testament, for example the age and authorship of its various books. Decisive appeal cannot be made to the self-witness of the Bible in every case concerning the canonicity of particular writings.[44] In the introduction to his commentaries on Hebrews, James, 2 Peter, and Jude, Calvin defended their canonicity in opposition to objections or doubts raised within the early church and in his own day. He did that not simply by appealing to the witness of the Holy Spirit as some infallible, inward arbitrator, but he appealed to the fact that the authority of those books has been recognized from the church's inception, that they contain nothing unworthy of an apostle of Christ, and that the majesty of the Spirit of Christ is everywhere apparent in them.[45] For Calvin, the decisive factor was agreement with the writings of the New Testament as a whole. Calvin's reasoning may be open to criticism, but he may not be accused of simply appealing to the testimony of the Holy Spirit in the heart of the individual believer as the real criterion of canonicity. Grosheide is quite correct to stress that the witness of the Holy Spirit may not be appealed to in cases of doubt or uncertainty to decide the canonicity of a particular book or part of a book, any more than we can appeal to this witness in our hearts to decide the inspiration of any particular book.[46]

Apart from the issue of the limits of the canon, the *nature* of canonical authority cannot be decided by a simple appeal to the authoritative impact Scripture makes or to the witness of the Holy Spirit. The witness of the Spirit teaches us that such authority exists and that it is a divine authority. But the way in which the New Testament canon embodies this authority and the qualitative and quantitative extent of such authority in the New Testament are questions that cannot be decided in terms of the impact that Scripture makes on the church and the individual believer. These questions must be dealt with in a broader context.

Greijdanus's treatment of the basis for the recognition of the canon seems unclear at this point. He affirms that Scripture itself must speak the

10

decisive word not only about the authority but also about the extent of the canon:

> The question as to which book is a part of Scripture and which is not is to be asked of the Scripture itself. In principle the Holy Scripture itself constitutes the basis for the acceptance of any part of Scripture as being the Word of God and for the rejection of any other text as Scripture. In this connection, too, Scripture shines by its own light; it is itself the source of our knowing its extent as well as its authority.[47]

We can agree with Greijdanus if he means that Scripture not only validates itself as canon but also, on careful investigation, sheds light on the nature and the extent of that canonicity. But that is not what he means. Repeatedly, he appeals to the authority that the various books claim for themselves in a material and formal sense. And he contends that a person has no alternative other than to accept or to reject this authority. He argues that the New Testament is such a unity that not to accept unconditionally even one book is necessarily to reject the whole of Scripture.[48] But in my judgment, no matter how correct Greijdanus's approach may be as it relates to the main content of the New Testament, Jesus Christ,[49] it is not an adequate grounding of the canonicity and inspiration of the New Testament as a closed unity, and Greijdanus is not able to provide a well-defined conception of the nature of inspiration and canonicity. He answers questions about canonicity and inspiration all too easily and exclusively in terms of the self-attestation of Scripture and the witness of the Holy Spirit, and he pays too little attention to the perspective of the history of redemption.[50] In my judgment, general canonics cannot simply rest on a general appeal to the authority of the New Testament and its claims to authority. Instead, it is necessary to determine, in the broader context of the history of revelation, the right of the church in receiving the twenty-seven books of the New Testament in their closed unity as canon and how in the light of that broader context this reception is to be understood.

Where, then, are we to find this wider context in terms of which we can arrive at a more exact concept of the canon and of its authority? Abraham Kuyper, in his discussion of general canonics as a theological discipline,[51] emphasized the need for such a wider context and insisted that both the Old and New Testament canons should be viewed in that light. He introduced what he called "the idea of the canon." According to Kuyper, God, the Lord, in opposition to the canon of the world, es-

11

tablishes himself as the canon. That notion of the "idea of the canon" may appear to be speculative and vague, but on closer examination it appears that Kuyper had in mind the history of revelation, in which Scripture not only emerges as a literary entity but where it also comes to the fore as canon.[52] Thus to form a correct concept of the canon of the New Testament, we must look *behind* the Scripture.[53] Naturally, that does not mean that we should go *outside* of Scripture to form a concept of the canon. It simply means that we cannot understand the significance of Scripture, of its canonicity and authority, apart from the context in which it arose, the history of redemption. In other words, it is necessary to examine more closely *the connection between the history of redemption and the canon.*

B. CANON AND REDEMPTIVE HISTORY

5. *The Apostolate*

At first sight, any interpretation that seeks to connect the history of redemption and the canon of the New Testament may appear to be forced. The New Testament certainly makes no mention of a canon as a closed unit of writings, and nowhere in the New Testament do we read anything about a mandate to compile a number of writings that would serve the church as a canon throughout history. It appears, then, that the idea of a canon arose and was adopted centuries after the great events of redemptive history—the incarnation, resurrection, ascension, and outpouring of the Holy Spirit—had occurred. Therefore it is not surprising that the contemporary literature in which the historical character of New Testament revelation is investigated so thoroughly pays so little attention to the significance of the New Testament as a written entity in the history of redemption. Because the New Testament Scripture appears to come into its own only *after* the great period of revelation, it is usually treated and judged as a phenomenon that belongs to the history of the church, rather than to the history of redemption.

But that is only a half-truth. The formation of the canon as a closed set of twenty-seven writings undoubtedly is a phenomenon that belongs to church history, not to redemptive history. The question, however, is whether or not the same thing is true of the canon in the qualitative sense of the word. Is what makes the canon the sacred and inviolable authority to which the church has bound itself and must continue to bind itself to be sought in the history of the church, or does it originate in the history of redemption?

12

The problem is not a terminological one about *canon*, a word that appears only a few times in the New Testament[54] (and then in a more general sense[55]). It is a question about the material authority the canonical writings had for the church from its inception[56]—authority that at least in the West determined the ecclesiastical use of *canon* to mean a standard, rule, and norm for faith and life.[57]

The material authority of the canonical writings originates in the history of redemption because in that history the unique work of Jesus Christ himself comes to light. In Christ, the one sent by the Father and the unique Son of God—and so the bearer of divine authority—God can be said to have revealed himself as canon over against the world. But the material authority of the New Testament originates in the history of redemption in another respect. For the *communication* and *transmission* of what was seen and heard in the fullness of time, Christ established *a formal authority structure to be the source and standard for all future preaching of the gospel*. From the beginning of His public ministry, we see Jesus intent on sharing His own power (*exousia*) with others so that this authority would take visible, tangible shape for the foundation and extension of the church on earth.

In that connection, *the apostolate* in particular should be noted. Jesus surrounded himself with twelve disciples whom He "appointed that they might be with him and that he might send them out to preach" (Mark 3:14). We are not able to examine every facet of this apostolate here,[58] but we can establish that the apostles' role in the history of redemption was unique and unrepeatable. Because they not only received revelation but were also the bearers and organs of revelation, their primary and most important task was to function as the foundation of the church. To that revelation Christ binds His church for all time; upon it He founds and builds His church.

The special significance of the apostolate in the divine plan of redemption is shown in many ways in the New Testament. The apostles are said to have been taken into the redemptive counsel of God about the sending of His Son. According to Acts 10:41, Peter said that from out of an entire nation God *chose* certain people (i.e., the apostles; cf. Acts 1:22, 26) to be witnesses to Jesus' resurrection, and in that way the apostolate was actually a part of God's redemptive activity in the fullness of time. Peter describes the significance of the apostolate in the history of redemption in more detail in Acts 10. According to Peter, the apostles are to give an authoritative and exclusive testimony in the world; they are to vouch for the truth and significance of Christ's redemptive acts.

13

The uniqueness of the apostolic office is also displayed in the expression "apostle of Jesus Christ." Recent research has shown that the formal structure of the apostolate was derived from the Jewish legal system, where one person could be given the legal power to represent another person. The representative who had such power of attorney was called a *shaliach* (apostle), and so unique was his relationship to the one he represented that the *shaliach* was regarded as that person himself. Therefore to receive an apostle was to receive the person who sent him. Jesus applied this formal structure to His apostles when He said, "He who receives you receives me, and he who receives me receives the one who sent me" (Matt. 10:40; cf. John 13:20). In another place Jesus said, "As the Father has sent me, I also am sending you" (John 20:21). Thus in an entirely unique and exclusive sense, Christ entrusted the gospel of the kingdom to the apostles because He commissioned and empowered them to represent Him. They were His instruments and organs in the continuation of revelation. They share in the mission of Christ himself, and together with Him they constitute the rock, the foundation, and the pillars of the church (Matt. 16:18; Gal. 2:9; Eph. 2:20).

The Holy Spirit endowed, prepared, and made the apostles competent for their task. According to Acts 1:2,[59] Jesus gave His commands to the apostles *whom He had chosen through the Holy Spirit*; their selection is attributed to the Spirit's work. The apostolate is not only the object of the divine counsel of redemption and the group representative of Jesus Christ, but it also has the Holy Spirit as its author. The Holy Spirit enabled the apostles to do their job. In addition to texts such as Matthew 10:18-20; Mark 13:11; Luke 21:13ff.; and Acts 1:8, of special importance are the well-known passages in the Gospel of John where Jesus promised His apostles that He would send them the Paraclete, the Spirit of truth, who would teach them all things, remind them of what Jesus had said, show them the way to the full truth, and also proclaim the future to them (John 14:26; 15:26, 27; 16:13, 15). We shall return to these passages.[60]

Here it is especially important to note the relationship those passages establish between Jesus' work, the Spirit's work, and the work of the apostles. Jesus says, the Spirit "will not speak on his own; he will speak only what he hears . . . he will glorify me by taking what is mine." In complete unity with Christ, the Spirit will continue to carry on His work; God's revelation in Jesus Christ continues by the operation of the Spirit. And as those fully commissioned by Christ, as the foundation of the church and as witnesses to what occurred in the fullness of time, the apostles were predestined, commissioned, and equipped for that continuing revelation.

Finally, if another typical statement about the special redemptive-historical significance of the apostolate is sought, one can point to Hebrews 2:2ff., where the revelatory witness of the apostles is compared to that of the angels in the Old Covenant. In the Old Testament—this is the writer's line of argument—the revealed word was spoken and made binding[61] by angels; so in the New Testament the redemption first announced by the Lord was *authenticated in a legally binding way* by the apostles who heard it.[62] The apostles were not simply witnesses or preachers in a general, ecclesiastical sense. Their word is the revelatory word; it is the unique, once-and-for-all witness to Christ to which the church and the world are accountable and by which they will be judged.

It is evident, then, that the New Testament itself inseparably unites the central events of redemption on the one hand and their announcement and transmission on the other. *The announcement of redemption cannot be separated from the history of redemption itself.* That proclamation was left neither to chance nor to human tradition or reporting nor to preaching, whether of religiously gifted individuals or of the church. Indeed, as apostolic proclamation, the announcement of redemption first of all belongs to the reality of revelation itself, and as such it has its own unique, once-and-for-all character. In that exclusive sense, apostolic proclamation is also the foundation of the church, to which the latter has known itself to be bound from the very beginning. It is the most holy faith on which the church has to build (see Jude 20; cp. v. 17), it is the pledge transmitted to it through the apostles, the *depositum custodi* (1 Tim. 6:20; 2 Tim. 1:14; 2:2) that the church has to preserve above everything else.

6. Tradition

We still have not reached a conclusive judgment about the form of the canon as it was accepted by the church, that is, as the twenty-seven books of the New Testament. Insofar as these writings were written by apostles (and not all of them were), we must realize that they were not the first and immediate result of the authority the apostles derived from Christ. The apostles initially exercised their authority orally, by preaching rather than by writing. When the apostles began to write, however, they placed their written words on the same level with their spoken ones. Paul, for example, writes, "Stand fast, and hold to the traditions which we have taught you, whether by word of mouth or by letter" (2 Thess. 2:15). In his epistles,

Peter also equates spoken and written apostolic words (cf. 1 Peter 1:12; 2 Peter 3:2), and in 2 Peter 3:16, on the border of the New Testament, so to speak, we already find clear traces of a collection of apostolic writings and of the forming of a written canon. Therefore to gain a correct conception of the New Testament writings, we must understand how, in general, apostolic preaching acquired its foundational significance for the church, and that requires us to understand the New Testament concept of *paradosis*, or tradition.

Generally speaking, every religion needs a tradition,[63] and the truth of this principle is reflected in the New Testament in many different ways. In the prologue of his twofold work (Luke–Acts), Luke appeals to the things that "were handed down to us by those who from the first were eyewitnesses and servants of the word" (Luke 1:1-4). Similarly, Jude exhorted his readers to contend to the utmost for the faith that was once delivered to the saints (Jude 3), a reference to the content for faith, developed in the rest of his letter. To give only one more example, among others, in his letters the apostle Paul never tires of reminding his readers of what he had once delivered when he proclaimed the gospel to them, either initially or subsequently (e.g., 1 Cor. 15:3; 11:23). Before we can speak of the New Testament writings as the church's canon, then, we must understand that in general *tradition* was the form in which the redemptive message of the New Testament was first cast, whether in its central meaning (Rom. 6:17; Col. 2:6ff.; 1 Thess. 2:13; 2 Thess. 2:15) or in its specific consequences for the life of the church (2 Thess. 3:6; 2 Peter 2:21). The New Testament does not have its full significance in and of itself. It is in part the precipitate and the fixed, written form of previous oral tradition. Together with this oral message of redemption, the New Testament initially belongs under the common denominator of tradition (2 Thess. 3:6).

Apostolic tradition, however, is not the stage at which the content of revelation moved beyond the reality of revelation and the history of redemption and became subject to the vicissitudes of ordinary human and ecclesiastical tradition. If such were the case, tradition, even in its written form, would not be the creation of Christ himself or the apostolic form of revelation that was established by the special direction of the Holy Spirit. Tradition would simply be the form that the Church gave to the gospel when all sorts of influences and contingencies became more and more difficult to control. It is in that latter sense that most scholars speak of the New Testament tradition, especially the synoptic tradition, and it is for those reasons that many people would examine the writings of the New

16

Testament according to principles that are applicable to human tradition in general.

The New Testament concept of tradition, however, has an entirely different meaning. In the New Testament, *tradition* does not refer to the general idea of historical traditions and legends as these appear among all peoples[64] or to the Greek idea of a particular school of thought as that is propagated in the schools of philosophy on the personal authority of teachers.[65] The New Testament's (especially Paul's) terminology for tradition indicates that the Christian concept of tradition was strongly influenced by the corresponding Jewish concept of tradition.

According to the Jewish understanding, the authority of a tradition was not derived from the forefathers or from some school but from the very nature of the transmitted material and from the corresponding office of the teachers of the law.[66] In Judaism, the content of tradition was constituted above all by the holy, God-given Torah, and those who were learned in the law enjoyed their authority because they "sat in Moses' seat" (Matt. 23:2). It is noteworthy that on the one hand, the traditions of the Jewish elders were rejected by Jesus and Paul as obfuscations of God's commandments and as misunderstandings of the redemption Christ brought (Mark 7:8 par; Matt. 5:21ff.; Col. 2:8, 16ff.); but on the other hand, the content of the Christian proclamation and its authority are repeatedly described by using the established Jewish terminology for tradition.[67] For example, when Paul urges the church to "retain"[68] and to "hold"[69] what he transmitted to it, he uses terminology that was currently in use by the Jews (1 Cor. 11:2; 15:2; 2 Thess. 2:15; cf. Mark 7:4-5, 8). Such terminology is especially evident in 1 Corinthians 15:1-4, the well-known passage about Christian tradition.

> Moreover, brothers, I declare to you the gospel which I preached to you, which also, you *received* (*parelabete*) and on which you stand; by which also you are saved, if you *hold fast* (*katechete*) what I preached to you, unless you have believed in vain. For I *delivered* (*paredoka*) to you first of all what I *also received* (*parelabon*), that Christ died for our sins according to the Scriptures, and that he was buried, and that he was raised again the third day according to the Scriptures.

The way in which these statements were influenced by Jewish terminology for tradition is shown by the italicized words. As he also does in 1 Corinthians 11:23, here Paul points to himself as both a receiver and a transmitter of Christian tradition. In both passages the use of "also,"

17

which implies "in turn," emphasizes that (1 Cor. 11:23, "what I *also* passed on to you" and 1 Cor. 15:3, "what I *also* received").

The nature of Christian tradition, then, is indicated by Paul's significant use of *delivered* and *received*. At present, many scholars think that in 1 Corinthians 15 Paul was citing a more or less fixed ecclesiastical confession of faith about Christ's suffering, death, and resurrection.[70] I believe, however, that the *paradosis* terminology places the emphasis elsewhere. The tradition of which Paul spoke was not social in nature; it did not find its setting (*Sitz im Leben*) in the collective activity of the church but was a manifestation of *personal* authority, namely the authority of the apostles. The apostles did *not* transmit the tradition only after it had been given a fixed form by the faith of the church[71] but because of the authority that they had received from Christ to be the bearers and custodians of this tradition. That such is the only proper understanding of Paul's concept of tradition is clear from the 1 Corinthians 15 passage, where he lists in succession the apostolic eyewitnesses who vouch for the content of the tradition mentioned at the beginning of the passage.[72] Their witness, not the belief of the church in some fixed form, determines the idea of tradition in the Corinthian passages. Luke uses the same line of argument in the prologue to his Gospel. The tradition to which he appeals and which he records in his Gospel rests on those who from the beginning were "eyewitnesses and servants of the word"—an indisputable reference to the apostles, as Acts 6:4 shows. It is in that light that we also must understand the character of the other synoptic Gospels. Mark 1:1, "the beginning of the gospel of Jesus Christ," must not be paraphrased to mean "the preaching of the community along the lines of Jesus"[73] but the preaching of the apostles that was delivered according to the commission they received from Christ.[74]

Thus the tradition of which the New Testament speaks is not an unchanneled stream that originates in great redemptive events and is then perpetuated as the faith or the theology of the church. Rather, it is nothing else than the authoritative proclamation that was entrusted to the apostles as Christ's witnesses and as the foundation of His church. It is a precious pledge that the apostles must transmit in exact accordance with their commission (1 Tim. 6:20).[75] Therefore the apostolic tradition is repeatedly called the *doctrine* to which one ought to subject himself in obedience (Rom. 6:17), or it is used as a synonym for such doctrine (Gal. 1:12; Phil. 4:9; Col. 2:6-7; 2 Thess. 2:15) and is equated with the apostolic gospel (1 Cor. 15:1) that one must not "receive" as the word of man but as it really is, as the Word of God (1 Thess. 2:13). We can ask whether this set of concepts, since it is used so frequently by Paul, always retains its original and full connotation, or whether it is sometimes simply used to mean "learning" or "instruction" in a general sense.[76] Even if the latter may be the case at times, that would not imply that the concept of tradition is thereby robbed of its special, authoritative sense and only derives its authority from the inner "vitality of faith" with which it is presented.[77] It is always the same apostolic authority that the apostle exercises when he frequently refers to his own preaching as that which is "delivered" and to the church's acceptance of it as that which is "received." It is this apostolic authority that makes tradition to be "tradition." Just as Paul, the former rabbinical student, once had unbounded zeal for the "traditions of the fathers" (Gal. 1:14)[78] because they were the holy traditions that the Rabbis traced back to Moses and thus to God, so he now pronounces a curse on anyone who preaches a gospel other than the transmitted gospel the church has received from him (Gal. 1:9).

* * * * *

The way Paul relates the transmission and preservation of the tradition to Christ brings all we have been saying into sharper focus. In Galatians 1, the passage just noted, Paul says that he did not receive the gospel he preached from *human* tradition[79] but through a special revelation Jesus Christ made to him (Gal. 1:12). For his authority to deliver the gospel, Paul appeals to the apostolic calling he has received from the living Lord himself (Gal. 1:15). But Paul did not ground the content of his apostolic proclamation and doctrine exclusively in the personal revelation he had received on the way to Damascus. Rather, when he speaks of the tradition he has received (1 Cor. 11 and 15), he undoubtedly indicates in the first place what he has heard from the other apostles.[80] Paul's listing of the eyewitnesses in 1 Corinthians 15 shows that such is surely the case. There was no conflict between the apostolic authorization Paul had received from the exalted Christ and using the tradition of other authorized persons. Paul was certainly not the only apostle, rather he was the last. Therefore, for his preaching he was partially dependent on what the other apostles had previously seen and heard (cf. 1 Cor. 15:8).

That does not alter the fact that Paul understood the entire tradition as inseparably related to Christ himself and that he even ascribed the transmission of the tradition to the living Lord. The way Paul introduces the tradition concerning the Lord's Supper is a particularly important illustration of that point: "For I [the emphatic use of *gar*] have received as tradi-

19

tion from the Lord what I have passed on to you, that the Lord Jesus. . . ." (1 Cor. 11:23).

The words "from the Lord"[81] are of special importance. Behind the tradition Paul received and passed on stood the Lord himself, and to Him Paul appealed in his awareness of his apostolic power ("for I") in opposition to the abuse of the Lord's supper in Corinth. Usually Paul's words have been interpreted as a reference to the Lord himself, to Jesus during His earthly ministry, as the first link in the chain of the transmission of the tradition about the Lord's Supper. On this view, the tradition Paul delivered to the Corinthians goes back to pronouncements from the earthly ministry of Jesus,[82] and so can be traced back to Jesus' own words.[83] This view certainly captures the important truth that in this passage Paul does not refer, as some hold, to a direct revelation he has received but to what has been communicated to him "horizontally" by other authorized bearers of tradition. Cullmann does not deny this appeal to authorized tradition bearers. He argues, however, that "the Lord" in 1 Corinthians 11:23 does not refer to the historical Jesus but to the exalted Lord, who sits on the right hand of God. According to Cullmann, then, Paul's formulation points to the present Christ, who stands behind the transmission of the tradition. So understood, this formulation is a direct communication from the Lord, without making it necessary to think of a vision or to exclude other bearers through whom the Lord transmitted the *paradosis*.[84] As the exalted Christ, the Lord is the bearer of the tradition; He stands behind the apostles, who transmit His words and deeds.[85]

Cullmann's argument commends itself because elsewhere when he apparently appeals to a word handed down from Jesus, Paul simply says "the Lord commands" or "the Lord says" (or does not say; cf. 1 Cor. 7:10, 12, 25; 1 Thess. 4:15). Tradition, therefore, can refer not only to an "historical" word of Jesus but also to a "direct" speaking of the Lord. Because of the form in which Paul communicated the tradition in 1 Corinthians 11:23,[86] it seems difficult to deny that his words at least include a reference to the risen Lord. In any case, one thing is clear: the Lord stands in back of the tradition, not only as the earthly Jesus but also as the exalted Lord. The explanation for this conviction is not only that Paul knew the earthly Jesus and the exalted Lord as one and the same person but also that he knew himself to be a servant who had been authorized by the heavenly Christ to transmit the historical words of Jesus. In Paul's mind, then, the transition between the different ways of describing tradition is fluid. Therefore tradition in the New Testament is more than just a reproduction of what once occurred. As apostolic tradition, it is the word of the living Lord; it is the authoritative word from Christ about Christ. It is the word that Christ himself employs, in the unity of His earthly and heavenly person, through the service of His apostles and through the Holy Spirit who has been bestowed on them (cf. 2 Tim. 1:14). Therefore anyone who listens to Christ's apostles hears Christ. Anyone who receives apostolic tradition must not receive it merely as man's word but as it actually is, as God's Word (1 Thess. 2:13).[87]

This concept of tradition seems to suggest that Paul saw no essential difference between what he received from others as tradition from the Lord and what in general he proclaimed to the church to be the word and will of the Lord. Some wish to draw this conclusion from the interchange of those two elements in 1 Corinthians 7 (cf. vv. 10, 12, 25, and 40). Paul says that he has no commandment from the Lord about virgins (v. 25). Although he does not use tradition in this context, commandment has the same meaning, as do "the Lord commands" and "the Lord says" in verses 10 and 12 (see above). That might suggest that the apostles appropriated to themselves absolute authority only insofar as they could appeal to words expressed by Jesus and that otherwise they only ascribed moral authority to their own words. In 1 Corinthians 7, however, Paul distinguishes between Jesus' own word that he has received as tradition and what he has to say to the church independently, on the basis of his apostolic authority, an authority that Paul claims comes from the Spirit of God (see v. 40, and cf. v. 25).

In 1 Corinthians 7 Paul is concerned with very special circumstances. He does not intend to make a general distinction between his own word and that of the Lord, so that he commands obedience for the latter but not the former. Rather, Paul wanted to make it clear that in some cases he could rest his appeal to apostolic authority on an express word of the Lord and in other cases he could not. Paul saw no difference between the authority of his own apostolic word and that of the words of the Lord that had been transmitted to him. That is clear from the fact that he repeatedly uses tradition, delivering, and receiving to refer to his teaching as a whole, and he does so in ways that make it impossible to discern the extent to which he bases his teaching on the words of the Lord that have been transmitted by tradition (cf. 1 Cor. 11:2; 2 Thess. 2:15; 3:6)—a state of affairs that is indicated by his fluid use of the terminology for tradition, as we have seen.

21

7. Tradition as Scripture

Finally, we may go one step further in determining what can serve as the redemptive-historical foundation of the New Testament canon. In the last section we discussed in general the concept of tradition in the New Testament, without distinguishing oral and written tradition, and we saw that the New Testament itself frequently ascribes the same authority to written tradition that it does to oral tradition (e.g., 2 Thess. 2:2, 15). A closer examination of some New Testament passages, however, indicates that the *written form* of apostolic tradition, in particular, is the form in which the (future) church would be bound to the apostolic word.

That was a natural development, unfolding by the very nature of the case. As time passed and the church spread across the world, the apostles could maintain contact with the various churches only through the written word. When the apostles died, oral tradition became less certain and therefore less trustworthy. That, in turn, enhanced the value and significance of the written apostolic tradition. Those developments are not simply deduced a posteriori from the subsequent historical facts. The New Testament itself indicates that the apostolic tradition was intentionally given in a written form so that it could be accurately preserved. First Corinthians 15 is such a passage. There Paul extensively and intentionally establishes the apostolic tradition about Jesus' resurrection by putting it in writing. He has not written anything new (v. 1). His concern is that the church retain the tradition in the *"words in which he had proclaimed it,"*[88] and for that reason he repeats those words in writing. Committing the apostolic tradition to writing settled once and for all the question of what had occurred, and it prevented further misunderstanding or falsification. This fixing of the apostolic tradition in written, ascertainable form finally led to a written canon.

Luke had the same reasons for communicating the apostolic tradition in writing. He carefully examined everything from the beginning and then wrote it down so that Theophilus might know with certainty those things he had heard about (Luke 1:1-4).[89] Committing the apostolic tradition to writing had the effect of strengthening confidence in its trustworthiness by "letting one know where he is." Fixing the tradition in written form tended to make it more precise. Subsequently, as the tradition advanced, this need for precision was hardly superfluous.[90] It has been correctly noted that the fixed, written form of the apostolic tradition is a fact of the greatest importance for the history of redemption[91] because it marks the

22

beginning of the distinction between oral and written tradition, a distinction that culminated in the formation of the New Testament canon.

There is more to be said about tradition as Scripture. Often the impression is given that the authors and initial recipients of the books of the New Testament did not consider these writings to be holy and canonical. If that were true, the question that a history of the canon would have to answer would be, "How did the New Testament books *become* holy books?"[92] Possibly, the same pregnant significance that the Old Testament possessed was not initially ascribed to the writings of the New Testament,[93] but two factors need to be kept in mind. First, all apostolic tradition, whether written or oral, had a special authority, so that the written form of the tradition as such had to have possessed such authority from the beginning.[94] Second, in a variety of ways the New Testament indicates how the authority of the written apostolic tradition was related to the authority of the Old Testament books. Paul intended that the initial recipients of his letters read them in the assembled church (Col. 4:16; 1 Thess. 5:27) in the same way that the writings of the Old Testament were read there. That helps to explain why the churches exchanged Paul's letters with one another. Similarly, Revelation 1:3 indicates that the Book of Revelation should be read in the churches.

The idea of a New Testament "Scripture" is expressed even more clearly in John's Gospel. The evangelist apparently applies to his own writings the promise of the Holy Spirit, who will lead and inspire the apostles in their witness to Christ (15:26-27; 16:13ff.).[95] Especially at the end of his Gospel, witnessing to Christ consists in "writing" (21:24), and the phrase "these things are written" functions to invite his readers to believe that Jesus is the Christ (20:30-31). In other words, the evangelist applies to his own book the *terminus technicus* ("these things are written") that he uses repeatedly to refer to Old Testament citations (John 2:17; 6:31, 45; 10:34; 12:14; 15:25) when in closing he summons his readers to faith in Christ.[96]

Because of the nature of apostolic authority and because of the meaning of the New Testament concept of tradition, it was natural to equate the New Testament as "holy" Scripture with the Old Testament. As we have seen,[97] within the history of the New Testament revelation the same divine sanction is ascribed to the apostles that the Old Testament ascribes to angels. Furthermore, in 2 Peter 3:2 "the commandment of your apostles" is placed on the same level with the canonical authority of the Old Testament prophets. According to Romans 16:26, by God's command the revealed mystery must be made known to all the nations by the prophetic Scriptures (of the Old Testament);[98] according to Ephesians 3:5,

23

through the Holy Spirit God revealed that same mystery to the holy apostles and (New Testament)[99] prophets. Therefore it is not surprising that the New Testament itself places Paul's letters on a par with the Old Testament Scriptures.[100]

Finally, nowhere is divine authority attributed to a New Testament writing more emphatically than in the Book of Revelation.[101] It claims to have been written under the direct command and leading of God (1:11, 19; 2:1ff.; 14:13; 19:9; 21:5). In the most solemn manner, it links salvation to reading, hearing, and keeping what is written in it (1:3), and it threatens to punish with the plagues it describes those who take away or add to its words (Rev. 2:18ff.). Nowhere else in the entire New Testament does the notion of the content of New Testament revelation being contained in a holy book receive a more impressive expression. In that respect the Book of Revelation no doubt occupies a special position among the other writings of the New Testament, and the authority it ascribes to the written word cannot simply be applied by analogy to the New Testament writings in general. Nevertheless, what the last book of the Bible states in a most explicit fashion and in keeping with its distinctive character illuminates an essential truth about the New Testament history of redemption: *God's authority as canon is not limited to His great deeds in Jesus Christ but extends to their communication in the words and writings of those He specially chose and equipped to be the bearers and instruments of divine revelation, and the written tradition they established, in analogy with the writings of the Old Testament, thereby became the foundation and standard of the coming church.* Therefore the redemptive-historical ground of the New Testament canon must be sought in that apostolic authority and tradition.

8. The Redemptive-Historical Concept of the Canon

If the preceding analysis of the redemptive-historical foundation of the New Testament canon is correct, it provides three positive and three negative perspectives that are extremely important for a correct view of the New Testament canon as it was accepted by the church. We will discuss the three positive considerations first.

(1) By accepting an objective canon as a final and absolute standard, the church acted in keeping with an important fact of the history of redemption. The church acknowledged that the authority Christ himself gave His apostles was an authority that made their witness and doctrine the church's foundation and norm.[102] Thus the canon that Christ's apostles gave the church (and which the church should accept as such) did

24

not come into being because the church itself instituted a standard to regulate its preaching and instruction; nor is the canon merely a record of what the early church believed. In its redemptive-historical sense, the canon is not the product of the church; rather the church is to be the product of the canon. Although the canon certainly shows what the apostles and the early church believed, its main significance is not that but that it embodies the revelatory Word of God.

(2) When understood in terms of the history of redemption, the canon cannot be open; in principle it must be *closed*. That follows directly from the unique and exclusive nature of the power the apostles received from Christ and from the commission He gave them to be witnesses to what they had seen and heard of the salvation He had brought. The result of this power and commission is the foundation of the church and the creation of the canon, and therefore these are naturally unrepeatable and exclusive in character. The closed nature of the canon thus rests ultimately on the once-and-for-all significance of the New Testament history of redemption itself, as that history is presented by the apostolic witness.[103] All the more, then, the New Testament cannot be qualified fundamentally as a witness to the faith of the early church. Such thinking not only fails to understand the revelatory nature of the canon, it also destroys the principial distinction between the canon of the church and the subsequent faith of the church. The closed character of the canon, in contrast, fully preserves this principial distinction between faith and revelation.

(3) The canon we have described could exist permanently only in a *written form*. Because at first there was no principial distinction between the oral and the written tradition (cf. 2 Thess. 2:15), for a time the closed character of the canon was qualitative in nature. What was canonical was limited to what was stamped with the special authority of Christ's apostles but was not yet quantitatively restricted to a fixed number of writings. The narrowing of the wider circle of oral and written canonical tradition became necessary, however, to safeguard that tradition against overgrowth by errors and legends. The New Testament itself, in fact, reveals that motive for a fixed, written canon,[104] and nowhere does this need make itself more strongly felt than when one reads accounts in the apocryphal gospels of the bizarre and arbitrary miracles the child Jesus allegedly performed. Thus the fact that from the beginning the church distinguished true from false tradition and was led eventually to accept a fixed, written canon happens by the nature of the case and has a clear basis in the New Testament itself.

The attempt to retain some form of ongoing oral tradition as a supplement to the written canon (as in Roman Catholicism) in fact relativizes the latter and makes illusory the church's intention in adopting the canon in the first place. By accepting the canon, not only has the church distinguished canonical from noncanonical *writings*, but it has established in general the limits of what it is able to acknowledge as the apostolic canon. The written canon, then, is the boundary between the history of redemption and the history of the church.

> The establishment of the Christian written canon indicates that *the Church itself* at a definite time drew a clear line of demarcation between the time of the apostles and the time of the church, between the time of the foundation and the time of the superstructure, between the apostolic church and the church of the bishops, between, in short, apostolic and ecclesiastical tradition. This occurrence would be meaningless if its significance were not the formation of the canon.[105]

Furthermore, the retention and development of an ongoing tradition alongside of the written canon presupposes an ecclesiastical authority that is competent to establish such a tradition and so, in fact, makes the authority of the tradition depend on the church (as is true in Roman Catholicism even for the written canon). Such a procedure reverses in principle the redemptive-historical order.[106]

In addition to those three positive considerations, the history of redemption also suggests these three negative conclusions that clarify the correct view of the New Testament canon.

(1) With the exception of the Old Testament canon, the New Testament recognizes no other principle besides apostolic authority and tradition that could have the same lasting, foundational significance for the church; in that sense, the New Testament recognizes only one canon. That point needs especially to be maintained in opposition to the thesis of Harnack and others that originally authority in the Christian church was primarily charismatic and exercised through prophets. Only later, he argued, when such pneumatic activities had ceased did the church's authority acquire an institutional and apostolic character. According to Harnack's famous statement, when the period of pneumatic enthusiasm ceased, the Spirit "was driven into a book,"[107] and Christianity was thereby transformed from a religion of the Spirit into a religion of the book.

Against that charismatic understanding of authority in the early church, one can point to the historical, once-and-for-all character of the

26

New Testament revelation of God. The canon for the Christian church goes back to and derives from that revelation, and above all else the canon consists in authentic preaching, witness, and teaching about what was once seen and heard. The various operations of the Spirit that occurred later in church history can never be substituted for or equated with the canon.[108]

According to the New Testament, no matter how influential such pneumatic voices and activities may have been in the early church, they did not have foundational significance for its origin. Only on the basis of the apostolic witness did such pneumatic operations have any place within the church, and in distinction from the apostolic witness, they had to be subjected to testing and criticism (1 Cor. 14:29ff.; 12:3; 1 Thess. 5:19ff.; 1 John 4:1). Grosheide has correctly observed that on the one hand the New Testament constantly requires absolute subjection to the apostolic word and never says that word is to be tested, though on the other hand such testing is required for the prophetic pronouncements of the prophets.[109] Therefore the prophetic gifts that emerged within the church cannot be placed on the same level with the powers with which Christ endowed His apostles. Likewise, it is erroneous to think that the apostles' authority gradually arose as a substitute for prophecy. The redemptive-historical foundation of the New Testament canon rests solely on that apostolic authority, and therein finds its qualitative limits.

Consequently, any attempt to subject the extent or content of the New Testament canon to the so-called spiritual criticism of the church violates the canon's redemptive-historical significance. Zahn, for example, in support of such criticism, appealed to passages that mention the gift of the Spirit to the church and the challenge to the church to distinguish the spirits, test everything, and hold fast to what is good (e.g., John 16:13; 1 Cor. 14:29; 1 Thess. 5:20ff.; 1 John 2:20, 27).[110] In those pronouncements, however, the church is plainly not being called to pass judgment on the unique authority of the apostles and so to place itself above the foundational authority Christ has given to it. Naturally, this observation does not yet prove that all twenty-seven books of the New Testament are part of that inviolable authority against which nothing can be said. But if the principle that the canonicity of its content is subject to the church's judgment of faith is valid for but one New Testament writing, a principle that Zahn apparently applies to all of them,[111] then the redemptive-historical concept of the canon can no longer be applied to the canon of the New Testament.

(2) In a modified form, such considerations hold against the view that reduces the canonicity of the New Testament to a specific core of preaching or to a *canon within the canon*. Of course what one accepts as a canonical core makes a significant difference. The fact that on the basis of such a principle of canonical authority one can appeal to the most divergent interpretations of the New Testament is sufficient to show the total inadequacy of this position to represent the redemptive-historical principle of power and authority. The authority to which Christ has bound His church and which the apostles as His representatives claim for themselves undoubtedly has a material character, that is, that authority does not refer primarily to a specific, precise formulation or codification of truth but to the apostolic tradition in general. The nature of this apostolic authority must be kept clearly in view (as I will subsequently show in detail). In itself Luther's principle of canonicity (*ob sie Christum treiben*, "whether they [the writings] urge Christ") is unassailable from a material point of view. Christ appointed His apostles as the foundation of His church with no other goal in mind. But Luther's principle should not be employed *within* the canon as a criterion of canonicity and thereby given the sense "whether and to what extent" something is canonical. In the final analysis, if the church wishes to remain faithful to the redemptive-historical nature of the canon, the question What does and does not "urge Christ" cannot be answered from outside the canon but only in accordance with it. The sole foundation of the church and at the same time its canon is Christ, and no one can or may lay another foundation (1 Cor. 3:11). But the way in which that foundation is formed and what properly belongs to it as "foundational" and canonical is not to be decided by the church, much less by individual believers. Their only task is to take care how they build on the foundation (1 Cor. 3:10). Therefore it is in fundamental conflict with the redemptive-historical nature of the canon for the church to seek a further criterion for distinguishing between true and false, between genuine and spurious. The canon is canon *suo genere* (uniquely), but it is also canon *suo iure* (in its own right).

(3) The *actualistic* concept of the canon is no less objectionable. According to this view, the canonicity of the New Testament consists in the church's hearing the Word of God in these writings, in different ways, again and again in the present as that happens repeatedly for the individual believer, each in his own way. If that view only emphasized that the canon has its effect on the church and on the believer solely through the operation of the Holy Spirit, then it would undoubtedly be compatible with the manner in which Christ has bound the power of the Holy Spirit

to the authority of the apostolic word and the witness of the Spirit to the witness of the apostles (John 15:26). But an actualistic understanding of the Spirit's work is erroneous because it implies that the canon has no existence or significance apart from the constantly recurring event of becoming the canon and the gospel. Such actualism reduces the content of the canon and of the gospel to what the church and the individual Christian understand *hic et nunc* (here and now) to be the gospel and the Word of God, thereby robbing the canon of its original redemptive-historical meaning, first by spiritualizing it and then by making it subjective.

It is true that what Christ has established as canon for His church can be duly received and recognized only by the operation of the Spirit, but that means neither that the canon (as the authoritative apostolic word) can be identified with such a working of the Spirit in the hearts of Christians nor even less, conversely, that what is canonical can be derived from what one momentarily believes he hears as the Word of God—an experience that may then be appealed to even *in opposition to* the written canon. The relationship Christ established in John 15:26 and 16:13ff. between the witness of the apostles and the witness of the Spirit makes the validity of this criticism indisputable. The apostolic witness is identical with the witness of the Spirit, not in the first place because the Spirit convicts *others* that the apostolic witness is true but because the Spirit has disclosed this witness to the apostles by leading them into the truth as they bore witness, by reminding them of the words of Christ, and by taking what is Christ's and making it known to them. Thus the redemptive-historical bond between the work of the Spirit and the canon is not to be found first of all in subjectively perceiving the gospel as canon but in its objective proclamation. In the categories of dogmatic theology, that bond is not provided by the illumination of believers but by the inspiration of the objective witness of the canon. Therefore to appeal to these passages in John in opposition to the New Testament's "it is written"[112] is totally mistaken, indeed the opposite of what these verses mean. At issue here is, in fact, the authority of what is written,[113] the authority of the apostolic witness as canon.

The foregoing rejection of an actualistic understanding of canon applies equally well to the belief that the promise of the Spirit in John's Gospel makes Christians independent from the canon's objective content, with its presumed contradictions, when they hear God's Word.[114] For the apostolic canon as the word by which others will believe is the *basis* of the church's unity (John 17:20, 21), and the notion of an internally contradictory canon is inherently absurd. Furthermore, Christ expressly stated that the Spirit would not speak on His own initiative but would take the things of Christ and proclaim them to the apostles. The content of the Spirit's testimony, then, is inseparable from that of the apostles, and the power the apostles received from Christ to establish their word as the church's canon was realized in terms of the Spirit's leading and inspiring them. Therefore to make the canonicity of the apostolic word dependent on the contemporary operation of the Spirit and to *oppose* the latter to the objective content of the apostolic word clashes head on with the redemptive-historical significance of the canon. It abolishes the once-and-for-all character of the history of redemption and leaves no place for the canon as its authorized witness.

To summarize, the starting point of Introduction to the New Testament (general canonics) is to ask what right the church has to accept a new collection of writings as holy and canonical alongside the Old Testament canon. Our provisional answer is that the church can and must do so. By giving authority to His apostles, Christ himself has given a foundation and canon to His church. This canon has an entirely unique, absolutely authoritative and closed character, and can be preserved only in written form. By accepting a fixed, closed collection of writings as exclusively canonical, the church has acted entirely in keeping with the structure and intention of the divine plan of redemption revealed in Christ. The Scripture that in this sense holds as canon for the church is therefore not to be regarded merely as a posthumous document of revelation but belongs itself to the process of revelation that occurred in the fullness of time. Scripture represents the witness of the Spirit that Christ promised would be combined with the witness of the apostles (John 15:26-27). Scripture is the rock laid by Christ himself and to which His statement to Peter applies in principle, "on this rock I will build my church" (Matt. 16:18).[115]

C. THE RECOGNITION OF THE CANON

9. *The A Priori of Faith*

So far we have discussed the redemptive-historical understanding of the canon. We must now return to the issue of the New Testament canon as a concrete collection of twenty-seven writings. This issue, one may say, is the real problem that any General Introduction to the New Testament must seek to settle: whether and on what basis the church has the right to accept *this* concrete collection of writings exclusively as *the* canon that constitutes the source of its preaching and its divine standard of faith and life. In other words, on what basis can it be established that this canon of

30

"the church" really represents the canon "of Christ," in the sense already discussed above?

If this issue is properly understood, what is at stake is the rightful place in the canon not only of those specific writings about which the early church and the Reformation had some uncertainty but also of every book in the New Testament. I have argued that the only demonstrable basis for the canon of the New Testament is the authority that Christ gave to His apostles and the accompanying assistance of the Holy Spirit promised to them. It is necessary, therefore, to show that not only a few disputed books but all the books of the New Testament have been produced by His apostolic authority and by the inspiration of the Holy Spirit. It is also necessary to show that certain other writings that circulated with the books of the New Testament—in some cases for a considerable time and very closely—were, nevertheless, properly excluded from the canon.

At first it might appear that the issue can be settled by simply applying the redemptive-historical principle of apostolicity and that in that principle we have an infallible criterion to test the canonicity of the individual writings. Modern investigations (we shall discuss the use of this "criterion" in the ancient church below[116]) have frequently argued that the touchstone of apostolicity (usually employed in a modified form) is adequate to establish the canonicity of the individual writings.[117] A closer examination, however, indicates that that path cannot be followed because we can no longer establish with historical certainty what in a redemptive-historical sense is apostolic and what is not. This uncertainty is due, in part, to the concept of apostolicity itself. Apostolic authority and apostolic tradition are by nature unique and circumscribed in their significance, but in the New Testament those concepts are not as sharply delineated as some passages appear to indicate; it is not possible *for us* to delimit them as clearly as we would wish. The *number* and *identity* of the apostles, for example, is unclear. There is a certain fluidity in the number of persons appointed by Christ to be apostles; the apostolate was not restricted to the historical twelve (a number that indicates a symbolic boundary), for Judas was rejected as an apostle and Matthias chosen in his stead (Acts 1:23-26), and later Paul was called to be an apostle (Acts 9:1-19; Rom. 1:1; Gal. 1:1, 11-24). And what are we to make of James (Gal. 1:19), of "all the apostles" (1 Cor. 15:7), and of the apostolate of Andronicus and Junias (Rom. 16:7)? Yet twelve continued to be the number used to refer to the apostles (Matt. 19:28; Luke 22:30; Rev. 21:14). Thus the apostolate was not distinguished and limited in terms of a number of persons (twelve or thirteen) but in terms of the nature of its work, which was to establish the church.[118]

It must be added that apostolic authority and apostolic tradition in the New Testament sense were not bound to the person of the apostle but gradually acquired an existence of their own. What is apostolic was not limited to the *viva vox* ("living voice") of the apostles or to their own writings but is also what is apostolic in subject matter and content, as the letters of Timothy and Titus demonstrate throughout. The apostolic witness authorized by Christ and inspired by the Holy Spirit became the *depositum custodi*, the pledge entrusted to the church (1 Tim. 3:15; 4:6, 12; 6:20; 2 Tim. 1:14; 2:2). Therefore Paul addresses the churches with others and through others (e.g., 1 Cor. 1:1; 2 Cor. 1:1; 1 Tim. 3:15). Thus even if the synoptic Gospels were not written by apostles, their content is to be received as the apostolic tradition and gospel (Luke 1:1ff.; Mark 1:1). That, however, does not deprive the apostolate of its unique, once-for-all character. Rather, it reveals how the apostles transmitted the foundation to the church. Therefore the question is whether a particular book has that apostolic and canonical significance for the church, whether its content embodies the foundational apostolic tradition, *not* whether it was written by the hand of an apostle.

It should be quite clear, then, that in understanding the redemptive-historical sense of apostolicity, we should neither restrict its meaning in too narrow a fashion nor receive *the historical judgment of the church* as to what is and what is not apostolic as the final basis for accepting the New Testament as holy and canonical. There is surely strong evidence of apostolicity for the majority of the New Testament writings. These writings bear the stamp of canonicity on their foreheads, as it were, and that evidence certainly forms one of the most forceful *motiva canonicitatis*. Conversely, to reject the apostolic authorship of certain writings, for example the Gospel of John, is difficult to explain, except as clear proof of an a priori, negative attitude about their content.[119] It is true, however, that not everything is apostolic that claims to be, as a single glance at the apocryphal literature will show. The Epistle to the Laodiceans, which is obviously nonapostolic, nevertheless begins with the same apostolic claims as the Epistle to the Galatians.[120] Between this positive and negative evidence, many instances are forthcoming where such clear evidence is lacking. Second Peter, for example, is not as evidently apostolic[121] as is 1 Peter or as is Paul's Epistle to the Romans. This state of affairs makes it clear that no matter how strong the evidence for apostolicity (and therefore for canonicity) may be in many instances and no matter how forceful the arguments in favor of the apostolicity of certain other writings may be, historical judgments cannot be the final and sole ground for the church's accepting the New Testament as canonical. To accept the New Testament on that ground would mean that the church would ultimately be basing its faith on the results of historical investigation. Although apostolicity constitutes the redemptive-historical foundation of the New Testament canon, that fact does not itself provide the touchstone and the criterion of its canonicity.

The canonicity of the New Testament, then, cannot be vindicated by historical investigation. Nor can it be justified by seeking the basis for the recognition of the canon in an authority that is external to it, which in an a posteriori fashion could then be the guarantee of canonicity. In particular, we have in mind here the Roman Catholic view that the authority of the canon rests on the authority of the church. Admittedly, Catholic theology explicitly distinguishes the authority of the canon *quoad se* ("as to itself") and *quoad nos* ("as to ourselves"), that is, the authority of Scripture in itself is not dependent on that of the church; only our acceptance of that authority, including recognition of the canon, is.[122] Nevertheless, it is difficult to reconcile that view with the redemptive-historical order because, for one thing, the church's authority is seen to have reference not only to the members of the church but also to the delimitation of the canon itself. By connecting the limits of the canon to the infallible authority of the church, the decision as to what is canonical depends on the church, and to that extent the authority of Scripture rests on that of the church. That, in effect, is a reversal of the redemptive-historical order, according to which the canon is not established by the church but the church by the canon.

But even where it is held that the church represents the authority of Scripture for believers, the church exceeds its competence by placing itself beside, if not above, the canon. That is not to deny that the church's authority has contributed a great deal to the recognition of the canon and will continue to have great significance for the progress of the faith. As Augustine said, "I would not have believed the gospel, unless the authority of the Church had induced me."[123] But if Augustine's remark is interpreted to mean that the recognition of the canon by believers rests on the authority of the church, then the church, in fact, usurps the place that properly belongs to the canon alone, thus, at the very least, equating its authority with that of the canon. The Roman Catholic idea is really that apostolic authority has been transmitted to the church and that the church is empowered by its head to make pronouncements about the canon, as well as tradition, that are themselves apostolic and canonical pronouncements. This notion we hold to be again in direct opposition to the history of redemption, in which apostolic power is entirely unique in character and is not capable of repetition or succession.[124]

Within the history of Protestant dogma as well, certain utterances have been made that appear to imply ecclesiastical infallibility with respect to the acceptance of the canon. It has been argued, for example, that the church received a special gift of the Holy Spirit to enable it to establish the canon by infallibly distinguishing divinely inspired from noninspired writings.[125] Protestants have also frequently spoken of the special providence of God with respect to the canon.[126] The loss of the one apostolic writing and the retention of the other, as well as the selection made by the church among the different writings, is then based directly on the special providence of God.[127] Sometimes the concept of the inspiration of Scripture has been extended to include the collecting and editing of Scripture itself.[128] Other Protestants have spoken of the assembling of the canon more in terms of the general leading of God's Spirit within His church, without implying that the church acted "infallibly" in this matter.[129]

Such statements contain much that raises objections, especially when they imply the infallibility and the inspiration of the church. To hold that the church could not have erred with respect to the establishment of the canon requires evidence. What is the basis for such a judgment? It is difficult to reconcile with the history of the canon.[130] From the standpoint of the Reformation, too, reference to the church's infallibility clearly was never intended to be understood as a *basis* for the canonicity of the New Testament. The very fact that such infallibility or inspiration is accepted solely with respect to the establishment of the canon and is thus to be qualified as an ad hoc inspiration or infallibility proves that the real order here is just the opposite. The canonicity of the New Testament has not been based on the assumed infallibility or inspiration of the church, rather the unquestioned canonicity of the New Testament led to such conclusions about ecclesiastical decisions. Such considerations, therefore, cannot help us to determine the ground on which recognition of the New Testament canon rests.

Another Protestant viewpoint is that the church's consensus about the canon arose of itself and so is the clearest proof that in establishing the canon, the church was guided by special providence; history itself, so to speak, offers the evidence for the canonicity of the New Testament. That consensus of the church, or rather that absolute authority acquired by the writings of the New Testament everywhere and without dispute, is then thought to guarantee the canonicity of these twenty-seven writings. The *providentia specialissima* is thought to manifest itself tangibly: not the church but the clear providential guidance of God in the formation of the canon confirms and attests (even if it does not guarantee) the canonicity of the New Testament writings.

That understanding of the relation of God's guidance, the church, and the canon, found in Reformed theology also,[131] contains an important truth (to which we shall have to return in detail): as far back as we can go, the authority of the great majority of New Testament writings has never been questioned within the church. Before there was a canon in the formal sense, these writings had already possessed canonical authority for a long time. Yet it is absolutely incorrect historically to imagine that the process of selecting certain writings and of rejecting others took place automatically without argument and debate and so bears visibly the mark of a divine work. It is an undeniable fact, for example, that James, Hebrews, and 2 Peter could not acquire general recognition until the fourth century, that until the sixth century the Syrian church rejected Revelation and of the Catholic Epistles accepted only James, 1 Peter, and 1 John, at the same time giving an apocryphal third epistle to the Corinthians a fixed place in the ecclesiastical canon. Furthermore, though the Book of Revelation was accepted in the second century as a holy book by all the churches in the East and the West, and though it was viewed as marking the boundary of the period of New Testament revelation (Rev. 22:18ff.), it was removed from the New Testament by the churches of Jerusalem, Antioch, Ephesus, and Constantinople, and it remained excluded for at least a century. Thus although it is entirely correct to emphasize the receptive attitude of the church with respect to the canon, the very history of selecting and closing the canon calls for extreme caution with respect to any appeal to this history as a witness to special providence in the canon's formation. Certainly the canon's history cannot provide the basis for its recognition by the church.

The matter is so complicated because the canon in its concrete form is the result of an historical development for which one seeks in vain after an a posteriori divine sanction. For no New Testament writing is there a certificate issued either by Christ or by the apostles that guarantees its canonicity, and we know nothing of a special revelation or voice from heaven that gave divine approval to the collection of the twenty-seven books in question. Every attempt to find an a posteriori element to justify the canon, whether in the doctrinal authority or in the gradually developing consensus of the church, goes beyond the canon itself, posits a canon above the canon, and thereby comes into conflict with the order of redemptive history and the nature of the canon itself.

Therefore it may appear that the only possible alternative is to seek the final ground for the recognition of the canon in the faith of the church or, more precisely, in the faith that the Holy Spirit produces and strengthens, by continual confrontation with the canon, in the hearts of those who belong to Christ. That means, in practice, that the internal witness of the Holy Spirit is the basis for the recognition of the canon. We have already[132] laid great emphasis on the necessity of this witness for the recognition of the divine authority of Holy Scripture. No historical argument, no recognition of the authority of the church, no appeal to the consensus of history, can replace, even to the slightest extent, the element of faith necessary for recognizing the canon. At the same time, however, we have agreed with those who argue that the witness of the Holy Spirit is not the *ground* for the recognition of the canon in its concrete form as a collection of twenty-seven writings. The witness of the Holy Spirit opens our eyes to the divine character of the gospel that encounters us in the writings of the New Testament.

But the witness of the Holy Spirit does not enable us with infallible certainty to distinguish the canon as such as a closed, concretely-fixed entity. In cases of uncertainty that continually arise with respect to the boundaries of the canon, the witness of the Spirit does not offer the church a pronouncement that serves as an objective basis for a decision. The witness of the Spirit accompanies the witness of the Scripture; it secures the acceptance and subjection to which Scripture lays claim. But the Spirit's witness does not clarify Scripture as Scripture, and it does not tell us why God's Word has come to us in this specific form.[133] Therefore the appeal to the witness of the Holy Spirit for the recognition of the canon is valid only insofar as the authority with which the Word of God speaks to us is ascribed to and identified a priori with the concrete canon. For that reason, however, the result of an exclusive appeal to the witness of the Holy Spirit has been that wherever the canon as such becomes an increasingly problematic entity, its authority is entirely or mainly limited to its *content*, and the authority of the canon as such is encumbered with ever greater reservations or is even abandoned in its entirety.[134]

In our opinion, appeal to the witness of the Holy Spirit for recognition of the canon may never be detached in a timeless, spiritualistic sense from the *historical* aspects of the canon; such an appeal must remain closely tied to those aspects. The ground for recognizing the canon does not lie in faith itself or in the witness of the Spirit who works that faith in our hearts but simply and solely in the a priori of the canon itself, that is, in the redemptive-historical reality that lies at the foundation of the canon as such and from which the latter springs. That reality precedes faith, the church, and the history of the canon. It lies most deeply in Christ himself and in the nature of His coming and work. The ground for the recognition of the canon is therefore in principle redemptive-historical, that is, Christological. Christ is not only himself the canon in which God comes to the world and in which He hallows himself before the world, but Christ also *establishes* the canon and gives it a concrete historical form. Christ establishes the canon first of all in His own word and work but then also in the transfer of authority (*exousia*) to His authorized representatives, in the Holy Spirit witnessing with them and through them, and in the apostolic tradition. And Christ is also the canon because He establishes and maintains the bond between that canon and the church. It is *this* rock (*petra*) on which He builds His church. The church shall be raised on this foundation; it shall have a canon no matter what it does with that canon. The church itself is not infallible, not even in its acceptance of what is and its rejection of what is not canonical. Nevertheless, Christ establishes the canon and continues to establish it, not only as a spiritual reality, not merely as a canon within the canon or as His current divine and infallible speaking in the human and fallible word of Scripture and the church. Rather, Christ establishes the canon in the ascertainable character of apostolic preaching and in the legibility of apostolic writings, in the preservation of the apostolic witness and doctrine. *Verbum Dei manet in aeternum* ("the Word of God abides forever"): not the Word in the word, not the Spirit in the Scripture, but the word as it was proclaimed in the church by and in the name of the apostles (1 Peter 1:25). It is the written word that as such began and shall continue its course throughout the ages. On that word and according to that canon, Christ will establish and build His church by causing the church to accept just this canon and, by means of the assistance and witness of the Holy Spirit, to recognize it as His.

What we have said does not have in view a specific church assembly or synod that at a certain juncture made pronouncements about the canon that have proven to be of great importance to the church of all ages. Such a gathering cannot prove itself to be, nor can it be proven a posteriori to be, preeminently or exclusively that church of which Christ spoke or to be temporarily gifted with infallibility. No ecclesiastical office, no ecclesiastical assembly, no matter how important, can pretend to guarantee the canon for the entire church and its future. For its acceptance of the canon, the church is always bound to Christ alone; it depends on Christ alone. By the same token, what Christ has promised with respect to the canon is valid for the entire future of the church. The canon of Christ will persist because there will continue to be a church of Christ, and the church of Christ will persist because the canon of Christ will continue to exist and because Christ through His Spirit will build His church on that canon. That is the a priori of faith with respect to the canon of the New Testament—an a priori that is based on the unity of Christ's earthly and heavenly person and work.

That a priori does not relieve us of the duty of investigating the history of the canon, and it does not give us the right, without further ado, to identify the canon of Christ with the canon of the church. The absoluteness of the canon is not to be detached from the relativity of history. It is true, however, that we shall have to view the history of the canon in the light of the a priori of faith; we shall have to view it as a history in which not only the power of human sin and error but above all the promise of Christ works itself out to establish and to build His church on the testimony of the apostles. Thus it seems that to continue to recognize the canon in its concrete form as the canon of Christ, we must combine both perspectives—the redemptive-historical a priori of faith and the history of the canon. It is naturally not possible here for us to describe the entire history of the canon, but we shall introduce what in that history appears to be of decisive significance for our present discussion.

10. The Formation of the Canon

The redemptive-historical background of the canon makes it clear that at first the church did not live exclusively by the Scripture of the New Testament. Rather, the church lived by the canon in the broader sense as that came through the apostolic word and the apostolic tradition, and that initial combination is clearly portrayed in the New Testament itself, where the apostles lay the foundation in their kerygma, witness, and teaching. The apostles delivered to the church the apostolic tradition, warned against false doctrine, and separated truth from error. The church received the tradition and teaching of the apostles orally and in written form, and lived by the one as well as by the other.[135]

Insofar as it depended on the written apostolic tradition, the church undoubtedly was not fully conscious immediately of living by a new Holy Scripture, though, as we have seen, the conditions for the latter were amply present in the apostolic tradition itself, and traces of it are to be found in the life of the church during its earliest period.[136] "Jesus" or "the Lord"[137] was cited, as were "the apostles," though they were not mentioned by name. Reference was also made to "the gospel," without meaning thereby the gospel writings in the formal sense of the word. However, the words quoted from "the gospel" in the earliest citations at our disposal (A.D. 90–140) nearly always appear to have been taken from our four Gospels.[138] On the one hand, then, it is evident that an exclusive and formal authority was not immediately ascribed to the written apostolic tradition. On the other hand, it is equally obvious that within the wider circle of the oral apostolic tradition, rather quickly the narrower, written tradition began to be delineated very clearly. That development is not to be explained in terms of conscious ecclesiastical activity that was preceded by deliberate reflection and reasoning. Rather, such a development proves that the church did not live nor did it wish to live by anything other than what it had received through the apostles in the name of Christ. To be able to *continue* to be sustained by that canon, as the wider circle of apostolic tradition became increasingly obscured, the church concentrated on apostolic tradition that was fixed in writing, the only form of that tradition it could utilize in the long run without hesitation. Irenaeus and Tertullian, for example, constantly based their appeal to Christ and the apostles exclusively on the *written* apostolic tradition.[139] By falling back on the written tradition, the church did not make a Holy Scripture; it did not proclaim something to be a canon. Rather, it established itself on its foundation, insofar as that foundation was available in a fixed form. The existence of the Old Testament Scripture and the way it was read in worship services and cited in general and theological usage undoubtedly exerted a gradual but noticeable influence on the formal structure of the authority of the New Testament Scriptures. Nevertheless, it was not the transfer of the authority of the Old Testament to the New but the original and inherent authority of Christ and His apostles that gave rise to the New Testament canon.

In that light, then, we must also reject the idea that the ecclesiastical canon was merely a reaction to the canon of Marcion or to the spiritualistic excess of the Montanists. It is well-known that about the middle of the second century, Marcion, a native of Pontus, separated from the church in Rome and established his own congregation. At Marcion's instigation, that congregation rejected the Old Testament in its entirety and as new Holy Scripture only recognized the Gospel of Luke and ten letters of Paul, and those in an abbreviated form, retouched according to the insights of Marcion. During the same period, all sorts of gnostic and pneumatic streams also arose that appealed to new revelations, created new gospels, and put into circulation the pronouncements of the "new prophecy" as holy tradition. Harnack, as is well-known, was the first to introduce the notion that the New Testament canon was assembled as an ecclesiastical countermeasure to offset these pneumatic and heretical streams.[140] Other scholars have gone further and argued that the church was forced to out-trump Marcion, so to speak, by positing over against his *one* gospel and ten epistles *four* gospels and a much more extensive apostolic canon, including Acts.[141]

Such an argument is overly speculative and does not agree with the facts. Marcion's canon was very clearly a reduction of what the church already held to be canonical; the canon of the church was not inspired by an idea of Marcion's (to introduce a "canon"). It can be shown that in Rome, where Marcion made his appearance, the majority of the New Testament writings had been recognized already (for a long time) as having an entirely unique authority.[142] It is true that we have no record of an underlying ecclesiastical decision that had precisely set the limits of that collection of writings, and it is also true that ecclesiastical practice during that period differed in various parts of the church in more than one respect. But such differences continued after the time of Marcion, and ecclesiastical decisions that made for uniformity in such matters, as far as we know, came much later (at the end of the fourth and at the beginning of the fifth century) and so can hardly be regarded as a reaction to Marcion. Such developments ought rather to be regarded as a "natural" (understood in a higher sense) development and not as the result of deliberate and planned ecclesiastical measures. There was never any discussion of the "canonicity" of the majority of the New Testament writings. The church never regarded those writings as being anything but the authoritative witness to the great time of redemption. The conflict between the church and Marcion was not concerned with the idea of a canon as such but with the limits and the content of the canon. It is certainly true, even self-evident, that the authority of books that were already universally recognized received sharper and more pregnant significance, both by the deviating manipulations of Marcion, as well as by the blurring of the canonical norms by the gnostics and Montanists. But that does not at all detract from the antecedent, de facto, self-evident authority of a large, substantial part of the New Testament and from the way, as far as we know, that authority has always been accepted by the church. The essence of the canon, not only qualitatively but quantitatively, is not an ecclesiastical product but one of the presuppositions of the church. In that sense, it must be said, the church did not create the canon, but the canon created the church.

By the same token, the church did not begin by making formal decisions about what was and was not canonical or by erecting specific criteria of canonicity. Rather, the way the canon attained its position of authority in the church is historical evidence that these writings were never understood by the church except as its foundation in the redemptive-historical, apostolic sense. For that reason, all manner of questions that have been formulated about the canon and announced to be the major problems of the history of the canon[143] are in essence pointless. That is the case, for example, with questions such as: "Why does the canon include four Gospels, not just one?" "Why did the so-called attempts of Marcion, the Ebionites, and Tatian to reduce these four to one gospel fail?" and "Why does the New Testament contain other writings in addition to the Gospels?" Such a complex of questions was never a matter of concern for the church as a whole. The church never made a decision between four Gospels and one gospel; it never decided to accept an apostolic canon in addition to the canon of the Gospels. The four Gospels and the majority of the Epistles simply formed the a priori of all its decisions, and for that reason all heretical, sectarian, or literary attempts to reduce the four Gospels to one already, a priori, had no chance of success. The fact that the four Gospels are not uniform and that there is a multiplicity within their unity (something that is even more true if one includes the Epistles with the Gospels) lends an even stronger emphasis to what we have been saying. The church never knew anything else than that *these* Gospels and *these* letters of Paul, among others, were what it could trust and what had been delivered to it as its foundation. The church was ignorant of any other foundation because (insofar as we understand something of the church's origin) it never had any foundation other than this tradition concerning Jesus and this teaching of the apostles.

Every effort to jar the church loose from its foundation (e.g., Marcion's attempt) or to erase its boundaries (e.g., the attempt of the Montanists) could only result in jolting it in its self-consciousness and existence as the church. Of course the church has used all sorts of arguments to *prove* the canonicity of writings that were under attack. Irenaeus, for example, attacked the introduction of new gospels by the gnostics and sought to prove the fourfold character of the Gospels by appealing to the four winds, to the four beasts mentioned in the Book of Revelation, and to the four covenants that God has made with mankind.[144] And the effort was repeatedly made in the Muratorian Canon and later to demonstrate the apostolic origin of the Gospels and of other writings under attack. As their artificiality indicates, however, those arguments are clearly a posteriori in character.[145] Saying that the church was ultimately led to accept those writings by certain *criteria canonicitatis* is, undoubtedly, to go too far.

41

Rather, it is clear that here we have to do with more or less successful attempts after the fact to "cover" with arguments what had already been settled for a long time and for which decision such reasoning or such a criterion had never been employed.

What concerns the initial and central composition of the canon ultimately is not the role that the *church* played or the authority that the *church* attributed to these books but the authority with which these books were given to the church as the foundation of her existence. Is that authority and that core of the canon, which as far as we know the church received unanimously and without contradiction, really the rock on which Christ promised to build His church, the foundation of the apostles and prophets? Or by accepting that gospel and that apostolic teaching has the church unwittingly followed the wrong course, so that in the final analysis what had been promised it is not what it has received? This question not only concerns the canon as a collection of writings but also strikes at the core of the content of the New Testament itself. Did Paul institute a "Christianity" that was different from that of Jesus? Do the Gospels, in which the figure of Jesus Christ is encountered, actually represent the canon in the redemptive-historical sense of the word? Do these books come to us with the authority of the apostles and as the testimony of the Spirit, or are they purely human and trustworthy only to the extent that human writings may be trusted? Should these books be investigated scientifically before we place our faith in them? Those are the real questions that lie at the heart of what is called General Canonics, or Introduction to the New Testament.

Here an effort can be made to oppose arguments with counter arguments. Some scholars believe that the writings of Paul and the Gospels no longer embody the original authority of Christ because at its very beginning all sorts of changes took place in the tradition. Such alleged alterations may be understood as "innocent" changes, or as many contemporary New Testament scholars argue, they may be regarded as a radical transformation of the original gospel. No matter how such changes are understood, we must press the question how they are to be accounted for historically. What is to be thought of those who went in and out with Jesus and who can hardly be denied the name *apostle*? The language of the New Testament already shows that they laid great emphasis on the trustworthiness of their witness to what they had seen and heard.[146] What are we to think of them, however, if they allowed what they really saw and heard to be transformed into an unhistorical and deteriorated complex of tradition, as many bellwethers of present-day New Testament studies would have us believe, even though they use the respectable term *kerygma* to refer to such distortions! If the apostles themselves are not guilty of transforming history, what then are we to think of the much discussed "theology of the church," which before their eyes and in their ears so radically transformed the original tradition in the two or three decades during which, everyone agrees, the material preserved in the Gospels received its essential form? Other than a ridiculous caricature, what would then remain of the New Testament concept of an apostle and of the holy apostolic tradition? And what would be left of the greatness and truth of Christ and of the power of His Spirit, other than an undetermined and uncontrollable current within the spiritual atmosphere?

Such historical considerations, however, no matter how reasonable they seem to us, are not the basis for recognition of the canon, and in actuality, they never have been. What caused the church to accept the central components of the canon as holy and canonical was the certainty that those particular books had been received from the hand of the Lord himself. And that again is the a priori of faith with respect to the canon; Jesus Christ cannot be separated from the canon; we can know Jesus Christ only in the manner in which He comes to us in the canon of the New Testament. It is equally true, however, that we cannot distinguish the canon correctly, except in the light of Christ, who is not only the content of the canon but also its great presupposition. Christ not only provides salvation, He also provides trustworthy communication about that salvation; that to the present day is the *principium canonicitatis*. Thus the question of the canon is not ecclesiastical but Christological. That position does not answer all historical questions in an a priori manner, not even with reference to the emergence of the original gospel. Nor does it provide a priori a doctrine of the canon and of inspiration. But for those who have faith in Christ, that Christological presupposition does vindicate the right of the church to accept as holy and canonical what it has received as the gospel and as the tradition of the apostles, and ultimately to set that canon apart and to distinguish it from all other writings.

11. The Closing of the Canon

Questions related to the limitation and closing of the canon have to be examined in the light of the preceding considerations. Once the church had received its foundation in what eventually became the center of the collection of New Testament books, it was inevitable[147] that sooner or later the limits of the canon would be established, and the canon would be closed. That outcome was all the more necessary to the degree that writings of doubtful origin and significance appeared. The actual historical process by which the limits of the canon were fixed was long and varied and cannot be described here in detail.[148] However, from the unconstrained statements of various ecclesiastical writers about the *homologoumena* (the writings that were universally recognized) and the *antilegoumena* (the writings that were opposed), it is clear that the variations and debates about the number of canonical writings played only a secondary role in the church and did not strike at its foundations, as did the conflicts with Marcion and the Montanists. That should not be surprising because in comparison with the writings the church universally held as canonical, the writings that were in question were only a few and were not nearly as important. In most instances, one cannot even speak of an explicit opposition to the books originally "opposed," for to a large extent differences were a matter of usage and not of principle. De Zwaan writes:

> We do *not* know of any real conflicts over a difference in "canon," and such conflicts certainly did not arise. It is also a fact that we can count on the fingers of one hand the instances where an appreciable difference in practice temporarily occurred.[149]

Uncertainty about *some* of those writings, it should be noted, only arose later, as a result of certain actions that occurred within or against the church. That is the case, for example, for two of the most widespread instances of uncertainty: doubt about the canonicity of Hebrews in the West and about the Book of Revelation in the East. Opposition to the Book of Revelation in the East, as is well known, was late in origin and was the result of dogmatic, antichiliastic considerations. Apparently, objections to the canonicity of Hebrews were not "original," nor did they occur primarily because its Pauline authorship was doubted. Rather, those objections were late and arose because of the Montanist appeal to Hebrews 6:4.[150] Indeed, the Book of Hebrews was already in use sometime between A.D. 90 and 100 by Clement of Rome and later was also cited by Tertullian. Moreover, as Van Unnik has recently demonstrated, between A.D. 140 and 150 in Rome all sorts of expressions from Hebrews were a part of the language of the church in the same manner as phraseology from other writings that were never contested in the West.[151] Thus here, too, it appears that only later reflection damaged the authority a document had from the beginning and destroyed the original certainty of the church.[152]

Thus on the one hand, every New Testament book did not initially enjoy an equally secure position as a part of the already existing core of the canon. Some books that were first accepted without opposition were later, in some parts of the church, the object of uncertainty.[153] On the other hand, that already existing canon exerted a powerful influence in the subsequent formation of the canon, in both a positive and a negative sense. When attacked by all sorts of heresies, the church's certainty about the writings it had received resulted in an even stronger, more persistent certainty. That strengthened certainty, in turn, made the church all the more critical of anything that deviated from those writings and, in some instances, even more critical than later appeared to be necessary.

What factors ultimately played a role in the closing of the canon? Undoubtedly, all sorts of special causes, including church politics, can be taken into consideration, both for the growing agreement between certain parts of the church, such as Rome, North Africa, and Alexandria, as well as in the case of the initially sharp differences between Rome and Alexandria, on the one hand, and Syria and Asia Minor, on the other. But closer examination indicates that all such special explanations and criteria of canonicity are insufficient. It has frequently been argued, for example, that ultimately what was of apostolic authorship was accepted and what was not was summarily rejected. That contention, however, fails to explain why the Epistle to the Hebrews was (again) finally accepted in the West, in spite of the fact that its Pauline authorship was most strongly doubted just by those who were most instrumental in gaining its acceptance, that is, by Jerome and Augustine. Another question, "Why was a very old writing like the Didache, in spite of its title claiming to be the teaching of the twelve apostles, not accepted?" And the same question can be asked about the alleged letter of Paul to the Laodiceans, which had a place in many manuscripts in the West and apparently around A.D. 600 was still accepted as Pauline by Pope Gregory.[154] In various ways, as also in the acceptance of the Revelation of John and the rejection of the Apocalypse of Peter, it appears that material, not formal, factors turned the scales.

If we survey the entire problem of the so-called *antilegoumena* and ask why some of those writings acquired a place in the canon and why others did not, it appears that ultimately two factors were always decisive.

The *first* factor was the growth of ecumenical ties between the various parts of the world church. Those ties made it increasingly evident that the rejection of some writings was confined to certain parts of the church and that the objections from an "orthodox" viewpoint to specific writings (e.g., Hebrews and Revelation) contradicted what had apparently been generally accepted in the larger church context for a long time. Thus when the Eastern Church came into closer contact with the Western Church, it was able to overcome its more recent objections to the Revelation of John. Similarly, when the Western Church became more familiar with the practice of the Eastern Church, it had to return to its original acceptance of Hebrews (and James?). And the churches of Asia Minor, and later the linguistically more isolated Syrian churches, had to abandon their rejection of the Catholic Epistles. The ultimate factor that again and again comes to the fore, both in the deliberations of leading figures and in the (few) documents that defend the final closing of the canon, is the attestation that the books, including many disputed ones, have been accepted by the church for a long time past.

That does not imply that the canon was closed by accepting either the lowest common multiple or the greatest common denominator of what was held to be canonical anywhere in the church. The facts run against both views. The canon is neither the result of an ecclesiastical survey nor of the consistent application of one or more formal criteria of canonicity. Rather, the impossibility of demonstrating such criteria shows that *besides* ecumenical contact, the factor that caused the church to reject or to accept a particular document was above all its *content*. In that connection we must always take into account the tremendous influence that the original canon, that is, the body of the canon that was never questioned within the church, must have had in shaping the judgments of the church and its leading figures. Only that influence can explain why writings such as the Epistle of Barnabas, the Shepherd of Hermas, the Epistle to the Laodiceans, and others were not universally recognized (though some sections of the church had used them early on), whereas Hebrews and Revelation were accepted. Similarly, James, 2 Peter, and 1 John were readily admitted later (though they did not originally belong to the body of the canon), thus at the same time paving the way for the other Catholic Epistles. In all of this, however, it would be a mistake to think that precise theological standards were adopted and applied as formal criteria of canonicity. Nowhere, for example, does one find a clearly defined reason for accepting James alongside the letters of Paul. The church retained its receptive attitude, but it knew what it had and in that possession found its power and direction, both in the defense and in the closing of the canon. The principial agreement and harmony of the various parts resulted in the canon as a whole. And those writings, which viewed by themselves and *suo iure* (in their own right) could not immediately secure universal acceptance, were, however, finally able to maintain their position because of their agreement with those writings whose place in the canon was undisputed.

Therefore, though the so-called closing of the canon was delayed for more than two centuries after the emergence of the core of the canon (in the so-called *homologoumena*), one may not make a principial distinction between what was immediately and universally accepted as canonical and what was only accepted gradually and later on. It is undoubtedly true that in the case of the latter, human decisions, ecclesiastical deliberations, and historical "accidents" played a much greater role than they did with respect to the main core of the canon, which established itself with irrefutable evidence as the foundation of the church. In our recognition of the canon, therefore, we must ultimately adopt the standpoint of faith that the church has, in fact, received its foundation secured by Christ. In the certainty with which the church has received the canon, church history "squares" with redemptive history. To the degree that the fringes of the canon were uncertain for a period of time and that debate, ecclesiastical strategy, and so forth were necessary to remove that uncertainty, we shall have to recognize, without abandoning our a priori of faith, that the decisions made with regard to the limits of the canon conform to the existence of the canon. In that sense one will have to understand and concur with Calvin's statements about several of the disputed books—statements that are frequently criticized but, in substance, are not so easily improved upon—namely that not only were such books accepted by the church from ancient times, but they also contain nothing that conflicts with the remaining, undisputed writings. *Sacra Scriptura sui ipius interpres*: Holy Scripture is its own interpreter. Does not that statement also contain an important truth about the boundaries of the canon?

CHAPTER II

THE AUTHORITY OF THE NEW TESTAMENT

12. *The Redemptive-Historical Character of the New Testament's Authority*

In chapter I we explored the intrinsic connection between the history of redemption and the canon of the New Testament. In doing so we not only discovered the foundation on which the New Testament canon rests, but we also gained a perspective in principle for properly distinguishing the nature of the New Testament Scriptures in general and the character of their authority in particular. The significance of that understanding can be further delineated from two sides.

On the one hand, what we have learned plainly reveals the inadequacy of every secular approach to the New Testament. A secular approach to the New Testament is one that begins by consciously abandoning the revelatory character of this written tradition. In the words of those who employ so-called historical-critical exegesis, such exegesis excludes the canonicity of Scripture, provisionally and hypothetically, and treats those writings as profane literature. It then leaves it up to the individual to decide whether or not the New Testament in its impact is experienced as a canon for faith and life.[1]

The objection to the historical-critical method is not that it is historical. In that respect it has brought to light many things that formerly were either unknown or too often neglected. The objection is that the origin of the historical method is secular, not revelatory. The historical-critical method thus misunderstands the absolutely unique character not only of the content of the New Testament message but also of *the manner in which it has come to us.*

On the other hand, the redemptive-historical character of the New Testament provides a more exact delineation of what Reformed theology means by "organic" inspiration, as contrasted to "mechanical" inspiration, which it rejects. Although it is not necessary here for us to discuss the extent to which that terminology adequately expresses what it intends to say,[2] we do need to understand that organic inspiration has in view the *historical* character of inspiration and is not a one-sided, spiritualistic concept. By the latter I mean any view that scarcely reckons with the special

49

characteristics and nuances that inspiration receives from the history of redemption. Instead, the concept of inspiration is filled with a preconceived notion of revelation—whether revelation is understood in an intellectualistic sense as a set of divine pronouncements that merely need to be organized into a fully rounded system of truth or whether revelation is judged in a spiritualistic or subjectivistic fashion by one's own experience of revelation.

The objection to *that* view is not that it over emphasizes the revelatory character of Scripture. In that respect it strongly opposes, at least in part, the secular view. The objection, rather, is that a spiritualistic notion of inspiration has no eye for the *history* of revelation. In other words, in inspiration it separates the work of the Holy Spirit from the work of Christ and from the incarnation of the Word.

Our concern, therefore, is not to synthesize the spiritualistic and the secular approaches to Scripture; they are mutually exclusive, and neither brings us to our desired goal. Rather, we should attempt to discover the redemptive-historical categories that enable us to discern clearly the nature, the content, and then the inscripturated form of the New Testament, as well as the nature of its authority. And we must learn to do all this in the light of the New Testament itself and according to its own standards.

On the basis of what we have already said about the apostolic character of the New Testament message of salvation, it is not difficult to point out a number of such categories. Three stand out at a first glance, as it were, and all three relate to the inscripturated content of the New Testament: *kērygma* (proclamation of redemption), *marturia* (witness to redemption), and *didachē* (teaching about redemption). We shall use these three categories to illuminate further what we have so far said about the nature of the authority of the New Testament Scriptures.[3]

13. Kerygma (Proclamation)

Kerygma, the proclamation and declaration of salvation, is the first category that we will examine to determine the nature of the New Testament tradition. *Kerygma* is the most typical designation of the character of the content of the New Testament, at least with respect to the primary meaning and significance of that content.

The noun *kērygma* is used relatively infrequently to describe the character and content of New Testament revelation. In the synoptic Gospels, for example, it only occurs in the so-called short ending of Mark, which speaks of "the holy and imperishable *kērygma* of eternal salvation." Paul uses *kērygma* frequently to indicate the act of preaching (1 Cor. 2:4; Titus 1:3), the content of preaching (1 Cor. 1:21; 15:14; 16:25), and the office of preaching (2 Tim. 4:17).[4] The verb *kērussein*, however, is used very often. It is used first to characterize the appearance of John the Baptist (Mark 1:4; Matt. 3:1; Luke 3:3), then of Jesus himself (Mark 1:38; Luke 4:18-19; Matt. 4:17; Mark 1:14ff.), and finally of the apostles (Matt. 10:7, 27; 24:14; Luke 9:2; Acts 10:42; 1 Cor. 15:12ff., etc.). The translation of this word group as "preaching" conveys only part of its specific meaning. At least when used to describe Christian preaching, *kērygma* and *kērussein* refer to the proclamation or declaration of something that is new and startling.

Gospel (*euangelion*) is often used in a way that is very close in meaning to *kērygma* and *kērussein* (e.g., Mark 13:10; 14:9; 16:15; Gal. 2:2; Col. 1:23; Matt. 26:13; 24:14ff.). In keeping with the Old Testament background in Isaiah 52, 61, and in other passages, *gospel* signifies the good news of the imminent coming of God to save His people, a message that the bearers of glad tidings have to announce.[5] "To proclaim" (*kērussein*) and "to preach the gospel" (*euangelizesthai*) are synonymous,[6] and *gospel* characterizes the content of New Testament revelation in the same way that *kērygma* does, that is, as the message of God's great reversal, as the redemptive intrusion of God into history.

When used to describe the New Testament revelation, *kērygma* and *kērussein* derive their central meaning directly from the content of New Testament revelation itself. Above all, that content consists of a new and decisive *event*, the coming of the kingdom of God, the dawn of the great time of salvation that God had promised and His people had long awaited. Thus the content of the kerygma is variously described as the kingdom of God (Luke 8:1; 9:2; Acts 28:31), as the acceptable year of the Lord (Luke 4:19), as Christ (Acts 8:5; Phil. 1:15), and as the baptism of repentance for the remission of sins (Mark 1:4; 3:3), all of which describe God's acts of fulfillment and consummation in the coming and work of Christ.

As many have pointed out recently,[7] the kerygmatic character of the New Testament does not receive equal emphasis throughout the New Testament. Other descriptions are needed to capture the essence of the New Testament message more fully. It is undeniable, however, that the basic character of the entire content of the New Testament is kerygmatic, for the great event of Christ's coming in the fullness of time dominates everything.

As the *proclamation of salvation*, the kerygma in its original form is found most clearly in the Gospels, which according to Mark contain "the gospel of Jesus Christ" (1:1), that is, the apostolic proclamation about the advent of the great era of redemption (cf. Luke 1:1-4). The Book of Acts should also be viewed from a kerygmatic perspective. Acts relates the sequel of what Jesus began to do and to teach (1:1). It really contains the kerygma of the exalted Christ, which is the continuation of His earthly activity.[8] The Epistles and Revelation are different, however, insofar as they represent the apostolic ministry of the Word at a more advanced stage. To the extent that they do not contain the kerygma in its original form, however, the apostolic Epistles are simply the explication, application, and *anamnēsis* ("recollection") of what was originally proclaimed to the churches as kerygma.[9] Thus the entire work of the apostles can be characterized as a witness to the resurrection of Christ (Acts 1:22, passim), and Paul could testify that he did not wish to know anything else in the church other than Jesus Christ and Him crucified (1 Cor. 2:2; cf. Gal. 3:1; 1 Cor. 1:17-18).

The increasing clarity with which the kerygmatic character of the content of the New Testament has been recognized in the last several decades has resulted in a revolution in the general evaluation of its significance and authority. Because the tendency to see the New Testament kerygmatically is particularly important for our present discussion, at this point we will permit ourselves a brief historical resume of the development of this viewpoint.

For a long time the kerygmatic character of the New Testament was entirely misunderstood by seeing the Gospels and the Book of Acts as primitive histories about the life of Jesus and the apostles and by viewing the remaining books, especially the Epistles, as entirely different, as dogmatic discourses that have departed greatly from the original gospel history. As a literary genre, the Gospels have no ancient parallel, and in no respect can their composition and structure be compared with the "lives," or biographies, of the great men of antiquity. Nevertheless, for decades historical criticism has been occupied with the Gospels as if they were such biographies. By following general historical methods, modern criticism has attempted to construct a scientifically responsible historical "picture of Jesus," or "life of Jesus," and so with the help of those methods to discover and circumscribe the revelatory character of the Gospels.

The inevitable failure of that method has become increasingly clear. To begin with, the Gospels obviously do not intend to provide a temporally and locally coherent and comprehensive description of Jesus' activity. More significantly, the general scientific approach to history is not applicable to the study of the Gospels because of their completely supernatural content. Insofar as it has not resorted to all sorts of rationalistic explanations of the events described in the Gospels, that scientific approach has resulted in an ever more tenuous and less coherent picture of the historical Jesus, a picture that has to be held together by all sorts of psychologizing and historicizing hypotheses and that is only a weak shadow of the gospel portrayal of Jesus.[10]

The historical-critical method has resulted in two responses. The first is radical criticism itself. Radical criticism concluded that on balance, little, if anything, could still be known of what is called the historical Jesus. Consequently, it ascribed the picture of Jesus portrayed for us in the Gospels to the dogmatic belief of the later church in Jesus as the supernatural Son of God, a dogmatic portrayal that provides us with nothing "historical." The second response, that of Martin Kähler,[11] ran parallel to the first but came from an entirely different direction. In the name of Christian faith, Kähler appealed again to the biblical Christ of the Gospels, rejected the so-called historical picture of Jesus that the critics had formed by many additions and subtractions to the Gospels, and declared that the Gospels do not present historical description but kerygma, proclamation of Jesus.

Kähler's reaction was entirely different from that of radical historical criticism. Kähler used *kerygma* to detach himself from endless attempts to reach the so-called historical Jesus along the path of criticism. To do so, he argued that the Scriptures, especially the Gospels, were not given to us as historical documents in the sense that historical critics have thought. The Gospels, Kähler maintained, were given as a message, as a proclamation about Jesus as the Christ. Therefore the Gospels do not summon us to a historical-critical investigation of what may prove to be reliable in the so-called life of Jesus, but the decision of faith, before which the gospel as the message of divine salvation in Christ places us, is the appropriate and adequate response to the summons of the gospel.

Kähler's reaction to the attempts made by historical-literary criticism to arrive at the real, historical Jesus was certainly correct and liberating in many respects. Kähler's antithesis that the Gospels are not biographies about the so-called historical Jesus but kerygma about Jesus as the Christ failed, however, to specify the relationship between that kerygma and history. To the degree that the kerygmatic nature of the Gospels is emphasized, it is necessary to put precisely *that* relationship beyond all doubt. Otherwise, the danger is not imaginary that the gap between the "biblical Christ" and the "historical Jesus" will become ever greater and that amidst fervor to retain the former, the latter more and more gets lost.[12]

Subsequent history has shown how readily Kähler's position has resulted in losing the "historical Jesus" to the "biblical Christ." The remarkable thing is that the radical criticism, against which Kähler wanted to safeguard the gospel, has increasingly appealed to him and increasingly widened the distance between the historical Jesus and the biblical Christ.[13] For many, *kerygma* has become a slogan that gives historical criticism free play on the one hand, though on the other hand, supposedly, it fully honors the decision of faith before which the New Testament as *kerygma* places us. As some never tire of repeating, the New Testament message is not concerned to increase our "historical" knowledge or to satisfy our historical interests but to confront us with the kerygma, the message of the divine event of salvation. Such confrontation, they say, does not come about in historical investigation but in preaching, for there the kerygma speaks to us, presses us for a decision, and so makes present the event of salvation. The real importance of the kerygma, then, is not in the communication of what *has* happened but in what *still* occurs here and now when the kerygma is preached. In that way, so it is thought, the contemporaneous redemptive character of the New Testament kerygma is maintained on the one hand, and on the other hand, the answer to the question about how that redemptive event took place in the past can calmly be left to historical criticism.

The concept of the New Testament as contemporaneous kerygma, it should be noted, appeals repeatedly to dialectical theology.[14] Dialectical theologians also give an entirely free hand to historical criticism, at the same time believing that they are able to respect the absolute authority of the speaking of God in and through Scripture. Here, however, we must make a very important distinction. Although the radical kerygma-theology of our day would make faith completely independent from the historicity of redemptive facts, theologians such as Brunner and Barth do not recognize such a divorce.[15] Karl Barth, who also wishes to see the historical-critical method fully applied to Scripture, has declared with respect to the resurrection of Christ and in opposition to Bultmann: "There may well be events that may be much more certainly real than the historian as such can establish. And we have good grounds to assume that to such events, above all, belongs the history of the resurrection of Christ."[16]

It is understandable, however, that both those who hold to a radical kerygma theology[17] and those who reject the historical criticism of the New Testament kerygma in principle[18] observe that such a procedure makes the relationship between faith and biblical criticism extremely problematic. On the one hand, free reign is supposedly given to historical criticism; on the other hand, the latter is checked halfway. On the one hand, supposedly faith is not detached from the historical facts of redemption; on the other hand, the New Testament account of those redemptive facts is not recognized to be historically unassailable.

It is undeniable that insight into the kerygmatic character of the New Testament, of both the so-called historical books and the letters, has resulted in a much more exact appreciation of the nature of the content of the New Testament and so also of its purpose, focus, and authority. That appreciation is especially important for the theological exegesis of the New Testament. The Gospels and Acts are certainly a very special type of history book. One can in fact say that it is not their aim to increase historical knowledge for its own sake, that is, to communicate a quantity of historical data that would supplement what is already known from history. And Paul's Epistles are not to be characterized as "theology," as if our goal is to gather together and arrange, as systematically and extensively as possible, what they make known about God, creation, man, the last things, and so forth. The New Testament does not direct itself to the "historian" or to the "theologian" in man; it has a much more practical and existential orientation in the sense that it takes hold of man's deepest being, his heart, the center of his self-determination, and places him before a radical decision—the demand of faith. That does not mean that the character and goal of the New Testament are soteriologically determined in a one-sided fashion. As central themes of the New Testament, God's glorification and self-justification undoubtedly underlie the idea of redemption.[19] That, however, does not change the fact that New Testament revelation is concerned with increasing not historical or theological knowledge as such but that knowledge that is necessary for a right relationship with God. That relationship the New Testament calls "faith."

To the extent that recent exegesis has returned to the kerygmatic understanding of the New Testament, it has undoubtedly placed the true nature of the content of those writings in a better light[20] and contributed to a more adequate exegesis of the New Testament. Enough emphasis, however, can never be laid on the fact that the content of the kerygma is "the great works of God" (Acts 2:11) that have been realized in the coming and work of Jesus Christ; the kerygma stands or falls with the factuality of the *historical* events of which it is the proclamation. To say, then, that the New Testament kerygma is a claim that urges a decision and that the kerygma does not intend to increase our factual knowledge or to clarify our understanding creates a false antithesis. It is just the knowledge of what has occurred, the communication of the saving work of God in Jesus

Christ, as that takes place in the gospel, that addresses us and urges us to make the choice of faith.[21] The kerygma, then, is abandoned as kerygma when one believes that the redemptive events that it announces coincide with the proclamation itself. Above all else, the kerygma is concerned with what happened once and for all, before us and without us that nevertheless is of decisive significance for us. Thus the nature of faith is determined by the redemptive event, as that has once taken place and is proclaimed in the kerygma; the nature of the redemptive event is not determined by what faith hears, or believes it hears, in the kerygma. That needs to be maintained as forcefully as possible against a kerygma-theology that believes that the meaning of the kerygma for faith can be made independent of the kerygma's historical content. If that were true, then the kerygma would be nothing more than the means to bring about a decision of faith, and the content of that faith would not be determined by the historical content of the kerygma but by one's particular presuppositions about human "self-understanding."[22] That would reduce the content of the kerygma to what such faith finds relevant, and the redemptive event of which the gospel speaks would become identified with what faith experiences during and through preaching.[23]

That revelatory character and authority of the kerygma, understood as just described, are closely bound together. In my judgment, it needs to be made increasingly clear that the deepest issue in the present conflict about the significance of the kerygma concerns the way in which New Testament *Scripture* is involved in the saving activity of God in Jesus Christ. Is Scripture only the human kerygmatic witness to God's great deeds in Jesus Christ that the Spirit uses? If Scripture, however, is nothing more than a human document that as such is subject to all the relativity inherent in human history writing, with what authority can one appeal to the New Testament kerygma as opposed, for example, to a subjectivistic or existentialistic interpretation of the redemptive facts? Such interpretation, for its part, also appeals to the kerygma found in Scripture for its understanding of God's saving work in Christ. How will *it*, in turn, answer the question posed by secular existentialists concerning why one should depend on the New Testament kerygma to hear the "Word of God" and why one could not also discover and acquire the transcendental "gift" of freedom along another path.[24]

Those two questions are inseparable. The revelatory character of the New Testament kerygma can retain its absolute significance only when it is based on the factuality of the historical event of redemption that it proclaims, and that historical event of redemption can retain its absolute significance only when the kerygma about it (as that kerygma comes to us in the *Scripture* of the New Testament) is taken up into and qualified by the absolute, once-for-all character of that historical event. This position is not merely a *postulate* of a faith that strives after guarantees and security. To hold fast to this Scripture-principle means nothing else than that we take seriously the bond between the Spirit and the kerygma, *as that bond is revealed in redemptive history itself.* For the Spirit was not promised in the first place to those who would *hear* the kerygma but to those whom God called and authorized to *speak* it for the sake of all future generations so that those who hear the words of the apostles thereby hear the Word of God. The New Testament kerygma is not revelatory and a part of redemptive history merely because and to the degree that through it God's Spirit repeatedly brings us into contact with the historical and present reality of God in Jesus Christ and in that way continues God's contemporaneous speaking in the world here and now. Rather, the kerygma is revelatory and a part of redemptive history above all because in *itself*, in its written form, it is the proclamation, prepared by the Holy Spirit, of the redemptive event that occurred in the fullness of time.

That naturally does not negate for a moment the fact that it is only by virtue of the work of the Holy Spirit that we share in the salvation proclaimed in the kerygma, and it does not mean that our faith is first of all in the authority of Scripture per se. Our faith is first of all in Christ, who comes revealed to us in the garb of Scripture, but that does not take away the inherent authority that belongs to Scripture as Scripture. Faith in Christ, as He comes to us in Scripture, teaches us to properly discern the authority of Scripture in its redemptive-historical significance.

The revelatory character and authority of the New Testament Scripture, therefore, undoubtedly has its bounds and limitations. Above all it has authority as kerygma, as the proclamation of the great redemptive works of God in Jesus Christ. To fulfill their calling as the inspired heralds of the redemption Christ achieved, the apostles did not share in divine omniscience, nor were they commissioned to reveal the mysteries of nature, to unlock the structure of the universe, or to solve the problems of science. Neither, then, is that the meaning and purpose of New Testament revelation in its written form. The New Testament is not a book of revelation in the sense that all of its pronouncements intend, directly or indirectly, to give answers to the questions with which life confronts us. It does not anticipate the natural development of the human race or the exploration of nature. It does not provide critiques of every time-bound conception of the structure of the universe and what takes place in it. It does not correct quotations from the Septuagint by making them agree with the Hebrew text, nor does it authorize every idea that Paul derived from his rabbinical training. Those qualifications, however, do not in any way detract from the revelatory character of the New Testament as *Scripture*, but they do teach us to distinguish its *nature*. And in doing so we should not make a dualistic or dynamic distinction between what has and what has not been written under the leading of the Spirit. As the New Testament Word of God, as the witness of the Spirit for the church and for the world, the entire New Testament is divine revelation. It is itself included in God's work in the fullness of time. But it is that above all in its kerygmatic significance, that is, as proclamation of the great acts of God in Christ. The New Testament, therefore, is totalitarian in its scope, touching every area of human life and knowledge, because the salvation of which it speaks is totalitarian. It has that scope, however, in its own way, that is, it illumines man and the world, history and the future, church and nation, the state and society, science and art from one standpoint, the standpoint of the coming, death, resurrection, and return of Christ.

All of what we have just discussed will become even clearer after we consider the further qualifications of the New Testament kerygma as *marturia* (redemptive *witness*) and as *didachē* (redemptive *teaching*).

14. Marturia (Witness)

Marturia primarily designates the content of the gospel in its original, historically *visible* and *audible* form. In the New Testament, *witness* above all refers to the communication of the ear- and eyewitnesses, to the communication of facts that were seen and heard.

The pregnant significance of this usage stands out all the more when we consider that the entire complex of concepts that is associated with *witness* and with *witness bearing* is juridical in origin and that the judicial meaning of these terms sets the basic tone of their New Testament usage. A witness of Jesus Christ is a person who has been commissioned by Christ to testify on His behalf before the forum of friend and foe—indeed before the whole of history—about what he has seen and heard. At stake in witnessing, then, is the relationship between authorization and fact; "the New Testament does not know of any witness bearing that is not bound to the facts."[25]

The New Testament's very strong emphasis on the character of the gospel as witness more precisely defines the concept of kerygma, as the overwhelming evidence (some of which follows) demonstrates.[26]

The concept of witness[27] is especially employed by *Luke* to characterize the proclamation of the gospel and to strongly emphasize the historical foundation of the kerygma.[28] In Luke's writings, witnesses are those who were *present* when Christ spoke and acted during His earthly ministry, especially after His resurrection, so that they are able to provide reports based on their own experience (Acts 1:22; 2:32; 3:15; 10:39; etc.), and they witness to that experience before the people. That witness, therefore, has both a receptive and a productive sense. In that dual sense, Luke explicitly includes Paul among the witnesses of Christ. Paul, too, though last of all, personally heard and saw the risen Christ, and because of that experience, Luke called him a witness (Acts 22:14ff.; 26:16). (Though *Paul* never called himself a witness of Christ, to support his apostleship he appealed to the fact that he had seen the risen Lord.[29])

The entire Gospel of *John* is governed by the concept of witnessing. John's programmatic pronouncement at the outset in 1:14, "The Word became flesh and dwelt among us," is directly connected with what had been seen by eyewitnesses, "and we have seen his glory." That corresponds with the farewell commission that Jesus himself gave to the eleven: "And you also shall bear witness, because you have been with me from the beginning" (15:27). Being a witness is repeatedly connected with seeing, with "having been with Jesus." "The one who saw it has given testimony, and his testimony is true, and he knows that he speaks the truth" (19:35; cf. 21:24). And at the beginning of John's first epistle we read—expressed with sweeping certainty—

> That which was from the beginning, which we have heard, which we have seen with our own eyes, which we have looked at and our hands have touched of the Word of life—the life was revealed and we have seen, and bear witness, and proclaim to you eternal life. . . . What we have seen and heard we declare to you, so that you also may have fellowship with us (1:1-3).

Peter also appeals to the fact that he is a personal witness when he exhorts the elders "as a fellow elder, a witness of Christ's sufferings"[30] (1 Peter 5:1). In his second epistle he says: "For we did not follow cleverly invented stories when we told you about the power and coming of our Lord Jesus Christ, but we were eyewitnesses of his majesty" (2 Peter 1:16). And according to Hebrews 2:3, to cite one final instance, salvation was first of all proclaimed by the Lord and then transmitted in a reliable fashion by those who *heard* it.

Such testimony occupies an entirely unique place in the history of redemption. Not everyone can become a witness, not even everyone who was a witness in a receptive sense to God's revelation in Christ. This testimony about Christ is the redemptive Word that God has prepared for the world once and for all. Only those whom God expressly called and equipped for the task (Luke 24:47ff.; Acts 1:8, 22ff.; 5:32; John 15:26ff.) appear before the forum of history as Christ's witnesses. To be a witness in that sense, then, is identical with being an apostle (Acts 1:21, 22, 26; 1 Cor. 15:9-11, 15; John 15:27). There is, therefore, a sharp distinction in principle between the New Testament concepts of *bearing witness* and of *confessing*. To bear witness is to confess, but to confess is not to bear witness.[31] A witness is a redemptive-historical figure, appointed by Christ to vouch on God's and Christ's behalf, in the great lawsuit against the human race, for the truth and reality of what God has said and done in Christ. For that purpose, Christ authorized and equipped witnesses in a special sense.

Those considerations are directly connected with the fact that the New Testament very closely relates the witness of the apostles and *the witness of the Holy Spirit*.

> And we are his witnesses of these things and so also is the Holy Spirit, whom God has given to those who obey him (Acts 5:32). He [the Spirit] will testify about me; and you also must testify, for you have been with me from the beginning (John 15:26-27).

The commission to witness, which for John, too, first of all means to bear witness to the *historical* revelation of God in Jesus Christ ("for you have been with me from the beginning"), was carried out with the special cooperation of the Holy Spirit. The Spirit made room for that witness, and it was He who bore witness in and through the apostles to what *they* had seen and heard. It was the Spirit who taught them all things and brought to their minds what Jesus had said to them (John 14:26). That should certainly not be understood to refer solely to the reproduction of Jesus' words but above all to their meaning and intention, though the words that the Spirit will announce to the apostles and cause them to remember will still be the words of Jesus (John 16:14). At issue is the witness of the apostles through the Spirit about the historical Jesus.

In that sense, the apostolic witness forms the link, forged by the Spirit, between the great redemptive event wrought in the fullness of time and the church to come. Therefore that witness is not only a witness to revelation but is itself a part of this revelation.

60

* * * * *

We must therefore understand the nature of the New Testament Scriptures and their authority for the church in the light of that understanding of witness, which the New Testament documents, especially the Gospels, present. What Mark calls the gospel—a characterization of the entire content of his book (Mark 1:1)—is at the same time *marturia*. Luke points expressly to the receptive and productive witness of the apostles as the foundation and norm of his Gospel (Luke 1:1-4), and the Gospel of John indicates in so many words that it is the written witness of Jesus' disciple (John 21:24). The same understanding of witness bearing also characterizes the Book of Acts. Because Acts witnesses to the conflict and victory of the gospel in a world that is alienated from Christ,[32] it is a witness to the continued working of Christ himself. Although the New Testament Epistles certainly build on the previously established witness, they still frequently refer to that original witness and forcefully repeat it against heresies that arose within the church. Paul's appeal to the fact that he and others were eyewitnesses to the resurrection of Christ is the great example of that. Paul identified the content of his witness with the main content of the apostolic kerygma (1 Cor. 15:3, "first of all"), and on that witness, as the foundation of his entire Christian preaching, he rested the full weight of his continued work in the church.

* * * * *

All of that provides a clear confirmation and further explication of what we have said in the preceding section about the kerygmatic character of the content of the New Testament. The kerygma of the New Testament is to be understood as the historical *witness*, authorized by the Holy Spirit, to the mighty acts of God in the fullness of time. Here again we see how both the secular approach to the historical narratives of the New Testament and the actualistic conception of what the New Testament means by *kerygma* touch the heart of the matter. The extent of the divergences between biblical and secular approaches at this point is illustrated by Bultmann's remark that it is fatal to faith to make it depend on human eyewitnesses, as Paul does in 1 Corinthians 15. Bultmann argues that the historical fact of the resurrection cannot be established by witnesses,[33] no matter how many; it can only be believed as it is present in the kerygma.[34] If Rasker's remark that the New Testament witness to what happened in the past "shares in all the relativity that is always inherent in historical

61

sources"[35] is in fact correct, then Bultmann's observation would be entirely true. But the situation is quite different if the New Testament witness, even in the historical sense under discussion, shares in another "always," namely that of the divine redemptive event to which it is the witness. And as we have seen, it is just that unique characteristic that is so strongly emphasized about the New Testament message as *witness*. The distinction between that witness and all earlier and later books, Christian or non-Christian, does not merely lie in the fact that the New Testament books "were written by those who themselves were witnesses and hearers of the original Word and the original deed of God in the once-for-all revelation in Christ,"[36] for such a view would ascribe to their witness *as such* nothing more than a human authority.[37] But the distinctiveness of the New Testament witness resides in the fact that as witness, too, it is a part of that revelation in Christ itself, and in that sense it, too, has a "once-for-all" significance. It is the witness, authorized by Christ himself and prepared by the Holy Spirit, to what was heard, seen, and touched of the word of life. That is what gives the New Testament witness its revelatory character and its significance as the foundation of the church. Here alone is the reason why it is impossible to be confronted with the act of God in Christ in any way other than through the New Testament. The inner necessity of that connection can no longer be maintained as soon as the New Testament witness is understood merely in an actualistic or spiritualistic sense as the Word of God or as the witness of the Holy Spirit.

It is true that to understand the witness of the New Testament as both the witness of man and the witness of the Holy Spirit presents us with a relationship (constituting a problem for the correct "doctrine of Scripture") that can never be entirely comprehended. That relationship must equally determine the historical investigation of the Bible, on the one hand, and the church's confession about Scripture, on the other. It has been said that the church's task is "to maintain the freedom of science with pride."[38] But that is a questionable statement for two reasons. First, it is not the task of any church to determine the freedom and limitations of science. Second, such a statement misunderstands the close relationship between the church's faith in Scripture and the scientific investigation of Scripture. In that relationship, science undoubtedly does not have authority over faith or faith authority over science; science is as little under the control of faith as science is able to provide a check on faith. Rather, the relationship between them is such that each can assist the other to understand the nature of their object of investigation. For our present discussion, that means that a scientific approach to the New

62

Testament is correct only if it recognizes the witness of Scripture, even in the historical sense of the word discussed above, to be the witness of the Holy Spirit. By the same token, every infringement of scientific investigation upon this quality of the New Testament witness causes it to misjudge its object and so to forfeit its character as genuine science. That also means that if scientific investigation denies the historical truth and reality of the New Testament witness to God's mighty acts in Jesus Christ, that investigation misunderstands the character of that witness, understood by faith as the witness of the Holy Spirit, and so makes it into a lie. Scientific investigation of the New Testament and faith investigate basically the same object, and that means that the discoveries of which science is capable can be of great significance for faith. But the results of science can contribute to a correct appreciation and interpretation of the New Testament only if they are subject to an understanding of Scripture as the witness of the Spirit. The only adequate scientific approach to the witness of the New Testament, then, is that approach that accepts its witness as the witness of the Holy Spirit.[39]

Thus the scientific study of the New Testament can undoubtedly teach faith to distinguish more exactly the nature of this witness of the Holy Spirit, for the Spirit's witness in the Scriptures takes place through the testimony of men. Rather than detracting from the character of the Spirit's witness, however, that points the way to a more precise determination of the quality of that witness. The fact that this human witness was taken up into the power and work of the Spirit and that the Spirit gave that witness the stamp of His authority in no way diminishes the other fact that *men* were witnesses, in a receptive and productive sense, of God's great works in Jesus Christ. Not only did the Spirit inspire men to speak and write what they had received from Him, but He caused them to speak and write what they as witnesses had *seen* and *heard* with their human eyes and ears. Therefore the written witness of the New Testament does not lose its human character. That is so not only because it is expressed in human language and writing but also because it is an *eyewitness* report and as such remains human, the fruit of a perception that was not infinite and of a reproduction that did not exceed the limits of human comprehension and memory. That explains, for example, why everything that the apostles saw and heard did not become a part of the apostolic tradition (cf. John 20:30ff.; 21:25). It also accounts for the many uncertainties in the New Testament about the sequence of events, the circumstances under which something was said, and the wording in which something was expressed.

63

The fact that the witness was not borne by a single authorized person but by a number of apostles should also be considered. On the one hand, that factor strikingly reinforces both the power and the content of the gospel witness; on the other hand, it also explains the diversity of the historical tradition found in the New Testament. Not every word that Jesus spoke on a specific occasion is transmitted in the same manner, not every event is recounted with the same precision, and not every historical setting is described with the same clarity. That such is the case is amply demonstrated by the synopsis given in the first three Gospels, even when examined with the greatest reserve. Numerous questions about historical and material ties arise that cannot be answered with certainty, but those uncertainties do not justify depreciating the witness character of the content of the Gospels. Those variations and divergences in no way detract from the trustworthiness of what the Spirit would teach us in and by the witness of the apostles. Anyone who accepts the Gospels for what they purport to be—the Spirit-authorized redemptive message of the witnesses of Christ—is not troubled by discrepancies in the scope, sequence, and form of the gospel material, for those differences do not violate the absolute qualitative agreement and clarity of the gospel witness. It is evident that such variety and divergency are not excluded by the fact that the Spirit made the witness of the apostles to be His own and to that end led them into all truth. It is therefore not the task of textual criticism or of exegesis to correct or to harmonize material that obviously was never intended to be so treated. The task of the text critic and the exegete is rather to identify the various modes of apostolic witness and in that light, shed by Scripture itself, to focus our attention on what the Spirit unmistakably intends to teach the church in and by the word of the witnesses of Christ.

Another, and no less important, consideration fits into the larger picture here. So far in this section we have shown that the New Testament concept of kerygma finds its more exact determination in the concept of *witness*. That, however, does not take away from the fact that the New Testament witness remains *kerygma*, preaching. That witness is neither a lesson in history nor simply a proclamation that informs us of certain facts but a message that calls us to faith and repentance. That is clear not only from the kerygmatic character of the New Testament's content but also from the concept of *marturia* ("witness") itself. When the New Testament speaks of *witness*, the word has different "levels" of meaning, as is true of so many concepts in the New Testament. *Marturia* not only means to bear witness to facts but also to what those facts *mean*. It is not only a witness to historicity but also to the meaning and truth of that historicity. The witness to the resurrection, to mention a primary example, is not only concerned with the fact that Jesus was resurrected from the dead and that His grave was found to be empty, but that witness is no less concerned to tell us that this Jesus is the Christ, the Son of God, and that His resurrection is the great turning point in the history of redemption. Present, then, in the concept of witness is an inseparable conjunction between bearing witness to the facts and bearing witness to the truth (cf., e.g., Luke 24:48ff.; Acts 10:42). "The witness to facts and the witness to truth are one and the same—the unavoidable result of the fact that the gospel presents a historical revelation."[40] That conjunction likewise determines the character and authority of the New Testament's witness.

That ambivalence in the New Testament concept of witness appears wherever the term is used. That is true in Luke—where the historicity of the redemptive facts stands out sharply in the foreground—as well as in the other books of the New Testament. In the Gospel of John, the character of witness as witness to the "truth" receives a very special emphasis. The factual content of the witness is certainly of great significance to John,[41] but his primary concern is to show more precisely the mystery that was revealed in the historical person of Jesus of Nazareth. Already John the Baptist had stated, "I have seen and testify *that this is the Son of God*" (1:34); likewise he "testified": "*He who comes after me has surpassed me because he was before me*" (1:15). Similarly, Jesus' works "testify" that *the Father had sent Him* (5:36; 10:25). In that sense we should also understand that the Spirit of truth, who accompanies and prepares the witness of the apostles, "witnesses" to Him (15:27) and that the apostles themselves "witness" (1 John 4:14). The witness of the Spirit through the apostles is one in which facts and their meaning coincide. It is information *and* proclamation; it is directed to both the heart and to the understanding. Such witness is directed not only to history but no less to *redemptive* history, as the testimony about the spear that pierced Jesus' side after His death illustrates: "The man who saw it has given testimony, and his testimony is true. He knows that he tells the truth . . . *so that you also may believe*" (John 19:35). On the one hand, that statement strongly emphasizes the factual content of this testimony; on the other hand, it is not simply the historicity of Jesus' being pierced but the redemptive significance of His death that makes that information into "witness." Throughout the entire fourth Gospel, those two components—the historical facts and their redemptive-historical interpretation—mutually determine each other (cf. 21:24, 25; 20:30).

That pregnant character of the New Testament witness also explains all sorts of things that appear to be defects from a purely historical point of view. The frequent vagueness of the gospel narrative along chronological and topographical lines is well-known. Moreover, one gospel writer arranges material differently than another. The same miracles and words of Jesus may be placed in different settings, and the same words are often given in a different version. Such variations are not attributable solely to the witness as historical communication in the sense described above.[42] They include intentional changes that are explicable in terms of the kerygmatic goal of that witness. Luke knew very well that Jesus' entry into Nazareth occurred after, not before, the miracles of Capernaum (Luke 4:23), but he reverses the order of those events for material reasons. Likewise, Matthew arranges the miracles historically in a different way than Mark (cf. Matt. chs. 8–9), though it is evident from the second part of his Gospel that Matthew was familiar with the sequence in Mark's account. In other places Matthew combines in Jesus' sermons words that were spoken on different historical occasions. Matthew 10:17ff. is an irrefutable example of that. If we may assume—and I believe that this has been established on solid grounds—that the synoptic Gospels did not originate independently, then we can gain a much clearer insight into the ambivalence of the revelatory witness of the New Testament. It is certainly necessary here to avoid premature conclusions and to remember that each evangelist introduces not only his own purpose but also his "own" tradition. Nevertheless, we cannot assume that where one evangelist communicates the same material in a shorter or longer form or in words other than those that are found in the other Gospels, he always presents another tradition. Rather, we must realize that the gospel writers wrote with relative freedom in presenting the witness they had received and in their use of each others writings. Their abbreviations and clarifications of traditions that already existed show that to be the case (cf., e.g., Mark 11:10-12 with Matt. 21:10-12; and Mark 10:18 with Matt. 19:17ff.). All of that may easily be understood in terms of the special nature and aim of the witness of the evangelists. Their witness does not intend to be a precise historical or administrative brief that tries to reproduce, in as formal a manner as possible, what was said and done but to be a witness that is directed to faith.

In no other evangelist is the ambivalent character of that witness more clearly in the foreground than in John. His reports of Jesus' words are strongly determined by the character of his witness as directed toward faith, a situation that must be judged in the light of John's own report of

66

Jesus' statement that the Holy Spirit would remind the apostles of His words, cause them to understand their true meaning, and thus take from what is His and make it known to them. Here the emphasis is laid not so much on the eye and ear witness of the apostles, and so on their own memory, as on their being led by the Spirit. What the apostles proclaim are the words of Jesus as the Holy Spirit has taken from what is His. No other gospel writer reports the redemptive facts more graphically, more realistically, and in a more antidocetic manner, extending even to the minor details of what the apostles experienced (cf., e.g., 19:25ff., 33ff.; 20:1-9, 24ff.), than John. Above all else, John directs faith to what took place and to the manner in which it took place (19:35). The power and the content of John's witness are not found in its completeness or in its historical interest in everything that occurred but in the certainty that faith can rely on what is described and told about those events (20:30, 31).

In that sense, then, the Gospels have been able to function for the church throughout the centuries as the infallible witness to Jesus as the Christ. In all their mutual diversity, they nevertheless speak the same impressive language; they display the same incomparable picture; they are what they are: historical description *and* proclamation.

* * * * *

That ambivalent character of the New Testament witness finally enables us to understand in what sense it lays claim on our faith. Its claim is not made solely in a secular sense, whereby everything would depend on the personal trustworthiness of the eyewitnesses, a trustworthiness that could only be established on historical grounds. Rather, its claim is made because the Holy Spirit himself bears witness in and by the words of the apostles, so that those who deny the trustworthiness of that witness oppose the Holy Spirit. It is not simply the case that the Spirit sets His seal on the trustworthiness of historical information, so that those who accept the factuality of the content of this witness satisfy its claim to faith. Rather, the New Testament witness is fully the witness of the Spirit only because the Spirit himself testifies through this word and convinces men that this word of testimony is the word of life (John 16:8).

For that reason, one cannot separate the two components that give the New Testament witness its specific character without destroying the witness itself. One cannot abstract the witness, as though it were simply a report of facts, from its call to put trust in these facts as *redemptive* facts. So-called historical faith can in no respect be a correlate to the New

Testament witness. Moreover, it cannot be said of this witness (anymore than of the kerygma that takes shape in this witness) that it is a proclamation of redemption that has validity for everyone, whether he (already) is aware of it or not or whether he (already) believes it or not.[43] Witness is "witness," or "kerygma," in the New Testament sense of the word, because it makes a claim to this faith; and because without this faith, there can be no participation in the salvation that it proclaims.

But no more fatal destruction of that witness is possible than when its historical content is evaporated into an idea or absorbed into what it means for faith here and now. The validity of what has occurred in history is independent of whether or not it is believed, though it only bears fruit in those who believe. Both the idealistic and the existentialistic interpretation of the gospel, then, in fact abolish the kerygma as such because they abandon its character as *marturia*. It has been rightly said that when faith in the historical uniqueness and particularity of the revelation of Christ is abandoned, Christianity is discarded on the same heap with the many abstract systems of ideas and faded religious experiences of the most general nature; the suprahistorical content that supposedly still remains is actually just as nonobligating and colorless as every vulgar myth.[44] Therefore it is difficult to see how such a "translation" of the gospel can be more compelling to modern man than the full assertion of the historical witness to Jesus Christ.[45] The main objection, however, is that such a view separates biblical revelation from its historical and factual content, thereby violating the very heart of the *marturia*-character of the gospel. The identity of the factual content and the redemptive significance of the apostolic *marturia* constitute the true nature of New Testament Scripture and so the norm of Christian proclamation and the basis for the Christian faith.

15. Didachē (Teaching)

So far we have discussed the content of the New Testament in terms of those qualifications that above all refer to the central event of redemption in the coming of Christ. These qualifications are mainly applicable to the so-called historical books of the New Testament, the Gospels and Acts. More than once we have noted that the other books of the New Testament represent a more advanced stage of revelation. Although they flow from and build on the kerygma and the witness to the mighty redemptive act of God in Christ, they are not to be described simply as *kērygma* and *marturia*. Dahl, for example, correctly states: "The central content of the epistles and of preaching to the church was certainly the same as that of the missionary message. But believers already knew that message. . . . It is for this reason . . . that preaching to the church was more a matter of recall, of reminding, than of proclamation."[46]

That is entirely in accord with the apostles' significance and task in the history of redemption. As witnesses of Christ, it was not only their task to lay and to be the foundation of the church; but because of their missionary calling, they also had the ongoing duty in the church of protecting and nurturing the sheep and lambs of Christ (John 21:15ff.), of building up His body and bringing it to maturity so that it might no longer be immature, tossed up and down, here and there, under the influence of every wind of doctrine (Eph. 4:11ff.). To carry out that task, they received power and authority, *exousia*, from Christ, as Paul expressly declares in more than one passage (2 Cor. 10:8; 13:10).

In keeping with those observations, we can see that the content of the New Testament message, in addition to being defined as *kērygma* and *marturia*, is appropriately described in many other ways.[47] For our purposes, it is not necessary to give an exhaustive treatment of all such concepts, but still we ought to comment briefly on several of them.

In addition to *kērygma* and *marturia*, the words *didaskein, didaskalia,* and *didachē* (the act and content of teaching) especially deserve our attention as a description of the New Testament word of God proclaimed by the apostles.

Teaching and *preaching* are frequently brought into a close relationship with each other. Jesus already associated those words (Matt. 4:23; 9:35ff.), and so did the apostles He appointed (Matt. 6:30, cf. vs. 12; Acts 4:2; 5:42; 15:35; 28:31). What *to teach* and *teaching* indicate thus stands in the closest relation to the great redemptive event that is proclaimed in the kerygma of the gospel; it belongs to the essence of the New Testament proclamation of redemption. In keeping with that, those terms are also used in a comprehensive sense—"teaching the things concerning Jesus" (Acts 18:25; 28:31), "teaching the word of God" (Acts 18:11)—when in general the object of that "teaching" is the entire content of the gospel (Gal. 1:12; cf. vs. 11; Col. 2:27; Eph. 4:21; 2 Thess. 2:15). In that sense, the absolute use of *teaching* must also be understood to refer to the activity of the apostles (Acts 11:26; Col. 1:28), and the same reference is present in other expressions: "the teaching of the apostles" (Acts 2:42), "that form of teaching which was delivered to you" (Rom. 6:17), "the teaching of God, our Savior" (Titus 2:10), "the teaching which is according to godliness" (1 Tim. 6:3), "the good teaching" (1 Tim. 4:6), "the sound teaching"

(1 Tim. 1:10; 2 Tim. 4:3; Titus 1:9; 2:1), and "the teaching" (1 Tim. 6:1; Titus 1:9; 2 John 9).

Rengstorf's view[48] that *teaching* is not concerned with the redemptive facts, with the proclamation of redemption as such, but with the Old Testament and the revelation of God's *will* (based on the revelation of Christ) should be rejected because it involves a false antithesis. It is true that frequently *teaching* and *to teach* are concerned especially with ethics, but it is impossible to find Rengstorf's distinction supported by New Testament usage. Teaching not only accompanies the kerygma (Matt. 4:23; 11:1); from the outset it refers to the content of the kerygma (Matt. 5:2; Mark 1:27; 4:2ff.; Acts 28:31; Gal. 1:12) and in part consists of the further explanation of the nature and progress of the accomplishment of redemption (Mark 9:31; 4:2ff.; Acts 18:25).[49] In the New Testament, the activity and content of teaching have a comprehensive meaning, as passages such as Galatians 1:12; Colossians 2:7; and Acts 18:11 irrefutably show.

Teaching, then, is distinguished from *kērygma* more by form than by content.[50] Although *kērygma* is the work of a herald, *didachē* belongs to another sphere of activity, the sphere of religious instruction. The form of Jesus' teaching closely resembles the Jewish form of instruction, as that instruction took place in synagogues (cf. Luke 4:16ff.; Matt. 13:54), in disputations (cf. Mark 12:35), in the association between a religious teacher and his disciples (cf. Mark 7:31; John 18:19; etc.), and otherwise (cf. Matt. 5:2; Mark 4:1; Luke 13:26; etc.). The main point, however, is that in that way the communication of redemption also takes place in the form of instruction, of material explanation, and of more detailed answers.[51] We can understand, then, that as the announcement of the gospel took hold during the missionary phase of gospel proclamation, the gospel, which at first had been designated as *kērygma* and *marturia*, increasingly came to be described as "teaching," as "good teaching," and so forth. That is supported by the Book of Acts and by the Pauline Epistles, especially by the Pastoral Epistles. In those places, *teaching* acquires in general the significance of instruction in the Christian faith, of the activity of Christian teaching, and of the content of that teaching (cf. Acts 11:26; Rom. 12:7; Col. 1:28; 1 Tim. 2: 12).[52]

All that happens by the nature of the case. New Testament revelation is communicated above all as proclamation of the word. Therefore, from the beginning, that announcement demanded that the meaning and consequences of that revelation be unfolded, that it be connected with preceding revelation, that it be distinguished from other religious views, and that it be defended against false teaching and heresy. All of that is amply found within the New Testament,[53] and it falls more under the concept of teaching than under kerygma. In that same sense, the New Testament also speaks repeatedly of "knowledge" (*gnōsis, epignōsis*) and of "knowledge of the truth," which frees one from error and ignorance (cf. Acts 17:30; Eph. 4:18; Col. 1:6; 1 Peter 1:14; 1 Tim. 2:4; Titus 1:1; Heb. 10:26; 2 Peter 1:3). Such knowledge is spread by preaching (2 Cor. 2:14; 4:6). With a slightly different nuance of meaning, it is also repeatedly referred to as "wisdom" (*sophia*) and as "insight" (*sunesis*) (Col. 1:9ff.). In short, New Testament revelation not only makes known the great and new event of redemption but in many different ways points to its implications.

It is difficult to describe in a few words what all of that includes. Whoever reads Paul's letters to the Romans, Galatians, or Colossians, as well as elsewhere, can form a picture of what is to be understood by this "knowledge of the truth" (*gnōsis alētheias*). That knowledge is not of a speculative nature[54] (Rom. 11:34; 1 Cor. 2:16) and is directly related to the practice of faith and life (1 Cor. 1:5; 12:8; etc.), yet that does not eliminate the fact that it advances by means of reasoning and theoretical reflection. Especially through studying the Old Testament, that knowledge achieves greater scope, depth, and clarity. In that sense, Paul repeatedly argues and draws conclusions (Gal. 3:7), brings the church to a deeper insight (Rom. 6:6), wishes also that the church "would be filled with the knowledge of his (God's) will, in all wisdom and spiritual understanding," and so forth (Col. 1:9ff.; cf. Rom. 12:2; Phil. 1:9ff.; etc.).[55] The writer of the Epistle to the Hebrews even distinguishes expressly between "the elementary principles of the oracles of God," in which the church has been instructed and which with a brief indication of their content he compares to feeding with "milk," and "solid food," the word that is more difficult to understand, in which the more "trained" must be instructed and of which in his epistle he provides a specimen (Heb. 5:11–6:3).

* * * * *

What has just been said also provides a new and very important element for determining the character and authority of the written word of the New Testament, an element that needs to be strongly emphasized, especially in opposition to the one-sidedness we have seen in the so-called kerygma theology. Knowledge has such a prominent role in the New Testament, not because already in early Christianity the intellect had overgrown faith or theology had overgrown conversion, but because knowledge is a direct result of the nature of the great works of God in Christ Jesus. That salvation is universal in nature; it encompasses man in his full existence and in all of his relationships and affairs, and it also dominates the entire past and future history of the human race, as well as that of the cosmos and the world of invisible things. The redemption described in the New Testament does not view all of that from the perspective of the empirically observable course of the human race in its fortunes, distress, and struggle for emancipation but from the great theocentric viewpoint of God's revelation in Jesus Christ. Thus there is the necessity of consciously connecting that revelation with the preceding history of revelation, of explaining what happened in Christ in the light of the Old Testament, and, conversely, of illuminating the Old Testament in the light of the event of salvation in Christ. From the very beginning, all of that is part of the "new teaching" (Mark 1:27; Luke 4:32).

That teaching is a core that emits its rays in all directions. On the basis of Christ's death, the New Testament also develops a "doctrine" of man, of his need of the way of salvation that has now been revealed, and of the believer's being comprehended in Christ from eternity past in the counsel of God (Eph. 1:4) to his glorification with Christ in the future (Col. 3:4; etc.). That teaching is what brings to light the hopelessness of the Jewish striving for salvation (Rom. 2ff.), as well as the darkness of heathendom in its fear of fate and demons (Col. 1–2). Because the entire New Testament is one great explication of the new event of salvation, the kerygma is also "teaching," and *pistis* ("faith") is also *gnōsis*—knowledge, insight, and wisdom. Thus the New Testament's authority is not only related to the one thing that it "proclaims" but also to the many things that it "teaches." It is a false antithesis to oppose faith in Jesus Christ, who is the Truth, to the possession of a "particular whole of conceptions and insights."[56] The apostolic teaching of the New Testament not only proclaims that in His person Jesus Christ is the Truth, but it also specifies with apostolic authority in what that truth consists. Certainly, that does not mean that New Testament "teaching" and "knowledge" provide us with a ready-made system of truth, so that to possess truth and to hold to sound teaching is a completely static and quantitative affair. The apostle Paul demands of the church an increase and growth in the knowledge of Christ, in whom the treasures of knowledge and wisdom are hidden (Col. 2:2ff.; Eph. 4:11ff.), and to that end he not only points the church to the person of Christ but also provides it with a material introduction to that knowledge and wisdom. He instructs the church in the Scriptures; he shows it the main lines

72

of the divine work of redemption; he teaches it to understand the nature of grace, the meaning of the law, and the origin and depths of sin; he explains to it the way of God with Israel; he unfolds the significance of Christ's death and resurrection in the light of the old covenant; and he describes the nature of the resurrection of the dead. When Paul so taught, he did not give his own theological speculations; rather he explained the mystery that had so far been hidden but was now revealed, and he did so with the same authority with which he had preached and testified to the reality of the event of redemption (cf. 1 Cor. 4:1; Eph. 3:2; Matt. 13:51).

Here we undoubtedly stand before the fact that this teaching about the universal significance of Christ is sometimes given in conceptions that were clearer and easier for the initial hearers and readers of the gospel to understand than they are for us. Naturally, that raises the question as to what is and what is not "taught" with the authority of the apostolic word. That there are reasons for such a distinction stems from the fact that the apostles' teaching comes to us in a language that is not our own and that must be translated for us to understand it. The problem, however, is more than a question of translation in the usual sense. Every language is an expression of the particular culture—the distinctive, time-bound ideas and conceptions—of which it is a part, and thus it is subject to change and disappearance because the ideas and conceptions it expresses change or disappear entirely. That is also true of the language and conceptions of the New Testament. For example, the manner in which the New Testament speaks about man in the various modes of his existence as soul, spirit, body, flesh, inward parts, and so forth is, on closer examination, sometimes untransferable into our own language, because the ideas that underlie those concepts are no longer our own. Thus the translation difficulty does not lie in the word so much as in the subject matter itself. That the communication of salvation as teaching means a "new doctrine" about man is undeniable, but clearly that teaching does not intend that the concepts it uses should serve to construct a "biblical psychology." The same may be said of the concepts and notions that the New Testament uses when it speaks of the cosmos. In its description of the cosmos, the New Testament uses the language and conceptions of its day. At times it expresses itself poetically; on other occasions it uses the current language of naive sense perception. Sometimes, however, it clearly alludes to or uses certain contemporary notions about the structure of the cosmos that are strange and difficult for us to assimilate, because they originate in a picture of the world that is different from our own (Phil. 2:10). The same is true, for example, when the New Testament speaks about demons in terms of conceptions derived from popular beliefs (Matt. 12:43;[57] Rev. 8:12; cf. Isa. 34:13, 14), and we encounter a similar problem in passages like Galatians 4:3 and Colossians 2:8, 19, which many understand in connection with pagan terminology.[58]

Those few illustrations clearly show that in dealing with the teaching of the New Testament, we are confronted by problems that are not to be solved or clarified by a few dogmatic pronouncements or by a single formula. Where and to what extent in that teaching can we distinguish word from subject matter, concept from teaching? The real problem here is the question of the *hermeneutics* (the theory of interpretation) of the New Testament: what does the New Testament *teach* us, what does the Holy Spirit, the author of the New Testament Scripture, mean? On the one hand, it is clear that in all sorts of ways the manner of expression and the formulation of the New Testament's teaching bear the mark of temporality, which is also determined by the capacity for comprehension on the part of those to whom that word was directed in the first place. Consequently, in many ways the New Testament's teaching is not intelligible to us without philological and archaeological knowledge (cf., e.g., 1 Cor. 11:10). On the other hand, it is equally clear that by using the form-content schema, it is possible to end up with the most radical reductions of the kerygma and teaching of the New Testament. The current demythologization of the New Testament is a most striking example of that kind of reductionism. By appealing to the dated "world view of the New Testament," those who demythologize explain as myth the entire history of redemption—the coming down of the Son of God into the world, His supernatural birth, His resurrection, ascension, and return.

Although we cannot treat here all the questions that arise from these comments, once again we must strongly emphasize the redemptive-historical character of the content and the authority of the New Testament. As we have seen, that redemptive-historical character holds true for the New Testament kerygma and marturia, and it holds true as well for New Testament teaching. The New Testament gives "knowledge," "insight," and "wisdom" on the basis of the one, unchangeable foundation—the mighty acts of God in Jesus Christ—and from that foundation light radiates in every direction, determining also the nature of the New Testament's teaching. That teaching is certainly not intended to provide us with all sorts of theoretical and practical teaching or insight, which as such do not proceed from the revelation of God in Jesus Christ. Thus the teaching of Scripture does not mean an end to all knowledge that goes beyond what was addressed to the first hearers and readers of the apostolic

74

word, and therefore an ongoing interpretation and application of the teaching of Scripture remains necessary. That, however, is not meant in any sense to introduce a sort of division of property between natural and supernatural knowledge, between faith and science. Precisely because of the redemptive-historical nature of the knowledge that the New Testament imparts, all things in heaven and on earth are, each in its own way, involved in its teaching. The revelation of God in Jesus Christ—who was before all things and by whom all things consist, both in their creation and in their re-creation (Col. 1:16ff.)—is the fulfillment of all His works (Col. 1:16ff.).

Therefore the question of hermeneutics cannot be how the kerygma and teaching of the New Testament can be "translated" in such a way that they can bring man to freedom on the basis of *his own* understanding of his existence in the midst of the world and history that surround him;[59] such an approach allows the teaching of Scripture to function only as far as it agrees with such a preconceived understanding of human existence. The history of theology makes embarrassingly clear the dangers that threaten us when the character and authority of New Testament teaching are consciously or unconsciously determined by the presuppositions of the spirit or philosophy of the time. For that reason the teaching and the nature of the authority of the New Testament cannot be explained by analogy from an extrabiblical schema or principle but only by the old Reformation rule, "according to the analogy of faith," that is, according to "the basic conceptions of Scripture as a whole."[60] For the New Testament that means, among other things, that its teaching and authority are not to be understood apart from the Old Testament, on which its "basic conceptions," deriving from the history of redemption, are based.

That is not to say that the teaching of the New Testament, with its various modes of expression, concepts, and ideas, is timeless. How great the breadth, and length, and height, and depth of what is revealed in Christ are can only be comprehended together with all the saints (Eph. 3:18). That revelation cannot be confined to the consciousness, to the language and comprehension of one individual, or of one generation, or of a single nation; nor can it be expressed only by the conceptual capacities of one particular culture. New Testament revelation continually calls for a new explication, a new understanding, a new expression, and it puts all human knowledge and development in their proper place by putting them under the light that in Christ has dawned on man and history. Therefore that revelation passes judgment on all human wisdom that would subject the authority of Scripture's teaching to its own autonomous standards and that would measure the meaning of that teaching accordingly. Recognition of the authority of the teaching of Scripture consists rather in "demolishing strongholds, destroying speculations and every tower raised up against the knowledge of God, and bringing into captivity every thought to the obedience of Christ. . . ." (2 Cor. 10:4-5).

Finally, we should remember that the characterization of the written word of the New Testament as *didachē* ("teaching") not only emphasizes its cognitive element but also refers to the edification of the church, in the comprehensive sense of the word. That teaching is also notably ethical in nature, and so it is described as the "holy commandment delivered unto them" (2 Peter 2:21), as well as the faith that was once delivered to the saints. Similarly, in Paul's letters, "teaching" can appear with "reproving"[61] and "exhorting"[62] (Col. 1:28; 3:16; 1 Tim. 6:2). In the New Testament *didachē* is also *paraklēsis*; the New Testament Word of God is also an ethical message. But that is not all. *Didachē* also has cultic and ecclesiastical implications, but we need not develop those themes here.

The preceding may suffice to illuminate the many different forms in which the one kerygma comes to expression and in which, then, the New Testament Scriptures appear. For that reason, then, the nature of the authority of those Scriptures is not to be expressed in a single word. Rather, the New Testament bears that authority as the one gospel whose authority derives from one central point—the activity of God that encompasses the world and history in the coming and the work of His Son, Jesus Christ.

NOTES

INTRODUCTION

1. Cf. A. Meyer, *RGG* (1909), 1.1208ff., s.v. *Bibelwissenschaft*; see E. Dinkler, "Bibelautorität und Bibelkritik" *ZTK* 47 (1950).
2. Cf. G. C. Berkouwer, *Het Probleem der Schriftkritiek*.
3. Cf. W. Schweitzer, *Schrift und Dogma in der Oekumene* (1953).
4. See, for example, S. Greijdanus, *Schriftgeloof en Canoniek* (1927), 29ff.
5. With respect to this "circle," see Schweitzer, *Schrift und Dogma*.

CHAPTER I

1. See, for example, A. Kuyper, *Encyclopaedie der H. Godgeleerdheid* (1909), 3.27ff.; F. W. Grosheide, *Algemeene Canoniek van het Nieuwe Testament* (1935), 28ff., 38ff. Others treat these questions under the history of the canon. See, for example, J. Th. Ubbink, *Inleiding tot de Theologische Studie*, ed. H. van Oyen (1946), 56, 61. Grosheide (*Canoniek*, 39, cf. 34) distinguishes (in our opinion correctly) between the question of the history of the canon ("What has authority as canon at a particular period?") and that of *general canonics* ("Why are the books of the New Testament canonical, and are they really canonical?").
2. For the Roman Catholic view, see pp. 26, 33–34.
3. H. Strathmann, "Die Krise des Kanons der Kirche, Joh. Gerhards und Joh. Sal. Semlers Erbe," *TBl* (1941): 295–310.
4. W. G. Kümmel, "Notwendigkeit und Grenze des neutestamentlichen Kanons," *ZTK* 47 (1950): 277–313, esp. 277.
5. For the views of Semler, see Strathmann, "Krise."
6. Thus, for example, Erich Dinkler ("Bibelautorität," 16) maintains that "in the 18th century, primarily through Lessing, Semler, and Herder, the idea of canon collapses, the idea that makes of the books of the Bible a unified collection of writings, separate from all other literature, and that, accordingly, must always call for and find a special exegesis for the entirely peculiar and wholly unique production that Scripture is."
7. F. Chr. Baur, "Die Einleitung in das N.T. als theologische Wissenschaft," *Theol. Jahrb.* (1850), 478.
8. A. Jülicher and E. Fascher, *Einleitung in das Neue Testament* (1931), 2.
9. Jülicher-Fasher therefore criticize the standpoint of Baur, "If one in principle (F. C. Baur, B. Weiss, H. J. Holtzmann), as the basic concern of New Testament Introduction, delivers a critical examination of particular a priori *conceptions* of the origin and collection of the New Testament documents, then the strictly historical character of such an examination becomes suspect, and a posterori conceptions about the New Testament are substituted for the place that belongs to the New Testament" (*Einleitung*, 4). This critique is thus also strongly *historical* in character!
10. See, for example, Kümmel's treatment of Luther's statements ("Notwendigkeit," 291–92; cf. A. D. R. Polman, *Onze Nederlandsche Geloofsbelijdenis*, 1.207–8).
11. Th. Zahn, *Die bleibende Bedeutung des neutestamentlichen Kanons für die Kirche* (1890).
12. Ibid., 48.
13. Ibid., 37ff.; 44.
14. Ibid., 27ff.; 46–47.

15. Ibid., 50ff.
16. Strathmann, "Krise," 309.
17. H. Faber, *Bijbelwaardeering, Bijbelgezag en Bijbelgebruik (Een Vrijzinnige bijdrage tot het probleem van de canon)*, 18.
18. Kümmel, "Notwendigkeit," 308.
19. Ibid., 305.
20. Ibid., 307.
21. Ibid., 309.
22. Ibid., 312.
23. Hermann Diem, *Das Problem des Schriftkanons* (1952), 13–14.
24. Ibid., 12, 15.
25. Ibid., 16, 23.
26. Ibid., 18ff.
27. E. Käsemann, "Begründet der neutestamentliche Kanon die Einheit der Kirche?" *EvT* 11 (1951–52): 13–21.
28. Ibid., 19. This judgment is quoted with approval by Bultmann, *Theology of the New Testament* (ET, 1955), 2.142.
29. Käsemann, "Kanon," 21. Similar views are also found in Dinkler, "Bibelautorität."
30. Cf. H. Bavinck, *Gereformeerde Dogmatiek* (1930), 4.428.
31. See, for example, J. Schniewind, "Die Schmalkaldischen Artikel und ihre Gegenwartsbedeutung," *Nachgelassene Reden und Aufsätze* (1952), 151.
32. The Lutherans speak of *per verbum* (the Reformed of *cum verbo*), cf. Bavinck, *Dogmatiek*, 4.437ff. The same thing appears to be meant when the *testimonium Spiritus Sancti* is included in the witness of the Spirit through Scripture. In opposition to this view (of Haitjema, Barth, and others), see Polman, *Geloofsbelijdenis* 1.224. Also see pp. 9ff.
33. Thus Diem, for example, holds that, apart from the "externality of the Word," justification is in danger of resting on something in man. *Sola Scriptura* is necessary to guarantee the *sola gratia* "in the proclamation process" (*Das Problem des Schriftkanons* [1952], 17). Kümmel goes much deeper into the "necessity" of the canon and affirms that faith in the *Einmaligkeit* (once-for-all character) of the revelation of God in Christ involves of itself insight into the necessity and the normative character of the New Testament canon. Because this revelation consisted of a unique historical event, only its written presentation by the first witnesses could be as uncorrupted as possible, and the collection of these words must necessarily become the canon ("Notwendigkeit," 297). Kümmel thus derives the necessity of the canon (correctly) from the unique historical character of the revelation, which as such can only be received and known by us in the form of communications of authorized witnesses. But the degree that this necessity is realized in the existing canon must be investigated a posteriori in a historical-critical manner. Also Käsemann does not wish to neglect the tradition retained in the canon. To do so would deny that God had revealed himself already before our time. Faith stands in history and in the continuity of the divine acts and the speaking of the Spirit. Only fanaticism can try to detach itself from this history ("Kanon," 21). The canon has thus become the report of the way that God has borne witness to himself in the past, not the normative Word of God for the present.
34. This is attempted by Zahn by requiring that the (imaginary!) judgment of the *entire* church be brought to bear on the canon (*Bedeutung*, 45; cf. Diem, *Problem*, 20). Kümmel ("Notwendigkeit," 310) seeks "the canon within the canon" in the central proclamation concerning Christ, by which the remaining witness of the New Testament can be measured. Käsemann apparently does not feel any need for such a "safeguarding" of the content of the canon (cf. the quotation in the text above, pp. 6–7).
35. Polman (*Geloofsbelijdenis*, 1.209) writes, "As far as we know the Basel Professor Musculus is the only exception. Among the books of the New Testament he notes some about which the opinion of the ancients differed, namely, 2 Peter, 2 and 3 John, Jude, Hebrews, and Revelation, to which the Epistle of James was added more recently by some. He does not

deem himself to be competent to determine whether these have been written by the authors whose names they bear. The judgment of the ancients weighs so heavily upon him that he feels less bound by these writings than by others, although he admits that he cannot readily find anything blameworthy contained in them." Also, see Polman's refutation (*Geloofsbelijdenis*, 1.209-10, 213ff.) of the opinion (of J. Cramer, J. A. Cramer, Barth) that Calvin adopted a critical attitude with respect to certain books of the New Testament. In our opinion, his refutation is sufficient.

36. Zahn, *Bedeutung*, 27-47.

37. Ibid., 35.

38. *Institutes*, 1.7.

39. Ibid., 1.7.2, "As to their question—How can we be assured that this has sprung from God unless we have recourse to the decree of the church?—it is as if someone asked: Whence will we learn to distinguish light from darkness, white from black, sweet from bitter? Indeed, Scripture exhibits fully as clear evidence of its own truth as white and black things do of their color, or sweet and bitter things do of their taste" (Battles translation).

40. Bavinck, *Dogmatiek*, 1.371.

41. K. Barth, *Die Lehre vom Worte Gottes* (1932), 1.110.

42. Cf. Bavinck, *Dogmatiek*, 1.567; S. Greijdanus, "Erkenningsgrond von den Kanon," *GThT* 14 (1913): 288; idem, "Anticritiek," *GThT* 15 (1914): 405ff.; idem, "Karakter van het *Testimonium Spiritus Sancti* volgens Calvijn," *GThT* 15 (1914): 419ff.; Polman, *Geloofsbelijdenis*, 1.233ff; S. P. Dee, "Het *Testimonium Spiritus Sancti* als subjectief principe van ons Schriftgeloof," *GThT* 30 (1929): 232ff.

43. Cf. the proof taken from the older Reformed theology in Polman (*Geloofsbelijdenis*, 1.232). Otherwise, Polman admits that the old theologians did not always distinguish so sharply in their terminology between ground and means (233).

44. Cf. Bavinck (*Dogmatiek*, 1.567), "Not the authenticity, nor the canonicity, nor even the inspiration, but the *divinitas* of Scripture, its divine authority, is hereby the proper object of the witness of the Holy Spirit." Also, Kuyper (*Principles of Sacred Theology*, ET, 1954) writes, that the *testimonium Spiritus Sancti* in itself does not have this content, "Hence it [the internal testimony of the Spirit] was a subdivision of the enlightening, but in this instance directed immediately upon the Holy Scripture, and not upon its inspiration, but its Divine quality" (557). "By itself it tends no further than to bear spiritual testimony to our personal, regenerated ego concerning the Divine character of everything the Holy Scripture teaches and reveals; and without more, the truth, for instance, of *graphic inspiration* can never be derived from it" (561).

45. Thus Calvin writes in the *Argument* to his commentary on Hebrews, "I ascribe it without contradiction to the apostolic letters, and I do not doubt that it is through the efforts of Satan that some have lowered its authority. For among the holy writings there is none that treats the priesthood of Christ in such a clear way." Calvin treats 2 Peter with more reserve. The style presents a special difficulty to him. And yet the letter contains in its entirety nothing that is unworthy of Peter. Indeed, it brings the power and grace of the apostolic spirit to full expression. If one accepts the letter as canonical, then one must also accept Peter as the author, not only because it bears his name, but also because it claims that its author lived with Christ. Calvin's conclusion is that although he does not recognize the style of Peter, he is in principle opposed to the rejection of the letter in its entirety, because in all parts of the letter the majesty of the Spirit of Christ appears in the foreground ("Doubtless, as in every part of the Epistle the majesty of the Spirit of Christ appears, to repudiate it is what I dread, though I do not here recognize the language of Peter"). In his *Argument* to his commentary on James, Calvin writes against those who do not ascribe canonical authority to it, "I accept it, however, gladly, without reservation, because I cannot find any legitimate reason for rejecting it." And even more, "It is enough reason for me to accept this letter that it does not contain anything that is unworthy of an apostle." With respect to Jude, Calvin writes that though there were disputes among the ancients concerning this letter, he willingly recognizes

it to be canonical, because it is profitable to read, and it does not contain anything that deviates from the purity of apostolic doctrine and was already recognized as authoritative from antiquity.

46. Grosheide, *Canoniek*, 21ff., 135ff.

47. "Erkenningsgrond van den Kanon," in *GThT* 14 (1913): 287.

48. Ibid., 285. See his *Schriftgeloof en Kanoniek* (1927), 29ff.

49. For example (*Schriftgeloof en Kanoniek*, 31), "The *believing* acceptance of Him (the Lord Christ) brought and brings of itself the believing acceptance of the writings, which make Him known in this way. . . . The Lord Christ and His being made known in our Gospels and the Acts of the Apostles are not to be separated. And they are related to each other in such a way that a choice must first be made with respect to the Lord, Himself, and this choice itself gives, and includes the attitude that is adopted with respect to the description of Christ" (32). What is especially of importance here is the meaning of the expression "of itself."

50. Although this is not lacking in Greijdanus (*Schriftgeloof en Kanoniek*, 35).

51. *Encyclopaedie*, 3.27–41.

52. Kuyper speaks of "the maturing of this idea in its historical process."

53. Grosheide (*Algemeene Canoniek*, 11ff.) also moves in this direction. In this context, however, Grosheide does not develop the redemptive-historical element. He limits himself to several statements that are more dogmatic in nature, "We have to remember that God cannot continue to reveal himself in Christ, as that occurred during Jesus' sojourn on earth. . . . And yet God's Word must still be heard. . . . Therefore it is necessary that if God is to continue to reveal himself as canon, what he has done must be described and his commandments recorded in books. . . . But the book that contains Divine revelation is also revelation itself" (*Canoniek*, 14–15). These more dogmatic statements find a detailed grounding in redemptive-historical data only later on in Grosheide's book, where he treats in a thorough way the historical development of the New Testament canon (41, 53).

54. Namely, in Gal. 6:16; 2 Cor. 10:13-16; and, according to some readings, in Phil. 3:16.

55. Cf. Gal. 6:16 (and Phil. 3:16), where it occurs in a principial sense as the norm of the new life in Christ. Beyer speaks of "the significant meaning that the term 'canon' has in the context in which it appears for the first time in Christian utterance" (*TDNT* 3.598).

56. Even if *kanōn* in its application to the writings of the New Testament originally meant something like "catalogue," or "list" (as this is also notably defended by Zahn, *RE* 9 1901: 769ff.), that would still in nowise prove the thesis of Semler that the canon was originally only an ecclesiastical cultic measure and did not represent a rule for faith.

57. Zahn (*RE* 9 1901: 771) also recognizes this. Beyer writes (*TDNT* 3.601), "Nor is the decisive point [of 'canon' as the description of the collection of holy Scriptures] the equation of *kanōn* with *katalogos*, formal though the use of the term may be. What really counted was the concept of norm inherent in the term. . . ."; cf. Grosheide, *Algemeene Canoniek*, 4.

58. See my article in *De apostolische kerk* (1954), 39–97.

59. At least according to the most probable exegesis. See, for example, Grosheide, *De Handelingen der Apostelen*, 1 (1942): 10.

60. See below, pp. 59–60.

61. *Bebaios*.

62. *Ebebaiōthē*, "made effective and shown to be valid by the apostles," H. Schlier, *TDNT* 1.603.

63. Bultmann, *Theology*, 2.119.

64. For this general idea, see, for example, *Webster's Ninth New Collegiate Dictionary* (1983), 1250, "(1) an inherited, established, or customary pattern of thought, action, or behavior . . . (2) the handing down of information, beliefs, and customs . . . from one generation to another . . ."

65. See, for example, Delling (*TDNT* 4.12), "In the Greek world the relation between teacher and pupil is largely controlled by personal confidence."

66. Cf. Delling, *TDNT* 4.12, and Kittel, *Die Probleme des palästinischen Spätjudentums und das Urchristentum* (1926), 64.

67. Cf. O. Cullmann, *Tradition* (1954), 8ff.

68. *Katechete.*

69. *Krateite.*

70. See, for example, O. Cullmann, *Die ersten Christlichen Glaubensbekenntnisse* (1943), 18; W. G. Kümmel, *Kirchenbegriff und Geschichtsbewusztsein in der Urgemeinde und bei Jesus* (1943), 3ff.; Bultmann, *Theology*, 2.121.

71. Thus (especially) Kümmel (*Kirchenbegriff*, 7), when he writes that we should conclude from 1 Corinthians 15:3 "that the primitive Christian community . . . is bearer of the decisive tradition concerning God's activity in Christ; therefore for the sake of this tradition one must adhere to the primitive community, if one wishes to maintain access to this divine revelation."

72. Cullmann, *Tradition*, 15ff., 25.

73. Thus Friedrich, *TDNT* 2.728.

74. "The Christ-tradition of the primitive Christian community exists as apostolic tradition," K. E. Skydsgaard, "Christus—Der Herr der Tradition," in *Schrift en Kerk* (presented to Th. L. Haitjema, 1953), 83.

75. Cf. Bultmann (*Theology*, 2.119), "The apostles' proclamation founded the tradition, and in the apostle concept the idea of tradition becomes the dominant factor." Cf. 105, "Thus the concept of the apostle . . . is primarily determined by the *idea of authorization*; his word is the word legitimized by the Lord. In addition to this, *the idea of tradition* gradually gains the preponderance, an idea which, of course, was not absent at the beginning (1 Cor. 15:3, 14f.)."

76. Thus, Delling, *TDNT* 4.13f.

77. Ibid.

78. Cf. Str-B, 1.691ff. (on Gal. 1:14).

79. *Oude gar egō para anthropou parelabon auto.*

80. See my *Paul and Jesus* (Philadelphia: Presbyterian and Reformed Pub. Co., 1958), 46–53, and Cullmann, *Tradition*, 15ff.

81. *Apo tou kuriou* (the most followed reading).

82. This would be expressed by *apo*; the preposition that refers to the mediating tradition is *para*.

83. "The Lord is the beginning point of the tradition," J. Weiss, *Der erste Korintherbrief* (Meyer, 9th ed., 1910), 283ff., quoted with approval by G. Kittel, *Probleme*, 64.

84. Cullmann, *Tradition*, 18.

85. Ibid., 20.

86. According to its form, the content of this tradition does not consist in the institution of the Lord's Supper itself but in the *report* about it that as such is not derived from Jesus himself but from the eyewitnesses. It does not say that Paul received information from the Lord about how He wished communion to be celebrated. Rather, it says, "I have received from the Lord . . . that the Lord Jesus in the night he was betrayed . . ." As appears from the repetition of the name of the Lord Jesus in the dependent clause, the tradition in this form did not come from Jesus himself but from the witnesses. As far as I know, Cullmann does not use this argument.

87. Cf. Skydsgaard, "Christus," 84ff.

88. *Tini logō euangelisamēn umin.* This rendering of this somewhat difficult expression seems the most acceptable. See Kümmel's (correcting) annotation in Lietzmann-Kümmel, *An die Korinther I-II* (1949), 191, "*tini logō* refers to the wording of the tradition already communicated by Paul to the Corinthians previously and . . . transmitted anew in what follows." This same translation is used by A. Friedrichsen (*The Apostle and His Message* [1947], 19), "[stating] through which word I announced it to you." The concern is the fixation of "the truth of the gospel" (Gal. 2:5, 14). Grosheide (*De erste brief van den apostel Paulus aan de kerk te*

Korinthe [1932], 490) understands *logos* primarily as the word according to its content, but he adds that those in error in Corinth probably used words that caused them to err and that Paul would not have wrong words do damage to the content of the gospel.

89. Since the plural *logōn*, not *logos*, is used, *katēchēthēs* probably should not be understood in the technical sense of religious instruction but more generally as receiving knowledge, as hearing (by rumor). By *logoi* we should understand the stories about Jesus that were in circulation. Thus, for example, S. Greijdanus, *Het heilig Evangelie naar de beschrijving van Lucas* (1940), 1.11–12; E. Klostermann, *Das Lukasevangelium* (1929), 3. Differently, H. Mulder, *Arcana revelata* (1951), 83.

90. See, for example, W. Manson, *The Gospel of Luke* (1945), 2; F. Hauck, *Das Evangelium des Lukas* (1934), 17, "In missionary and congregational activity, the Book of Luke sharply delimits the reliability of Christian traditional materials from merely fictitious stories."

91. Cf. Cullmann, *Tradition*, 43ff.

92. See, for example, the title of the writing of H. Lietzmann, *Wie wurden die Bücher des Neuen Testaments heilige Schrift?* (1907); cf. J. Leipoldt, *Geschichte des neutestamentlichen Kanons* (1907), 1.v.

93. Thus, for example, Schrenk, *TDNT* 1.745.

94. J. Gresham Machen, for example, correctly writes in *The Princeton Theological Review* (October 1923): 649, "It should never be forgotten that the Epistles of Paul were written consciously in the plenitude of apostolic authority. Their authority, like the authority of other New Testament books, was not something merely attributed to them subsequently by the church, but was inherent in them from the beginning."

95. Thus also Bultmann, *Das Evangelium des Johannes* (1950), 444. Also H. Windisch (*Johannes und die Synoptiker* [1926], 149) points to the "Paraclete sayings" as proof that "the intention and the conviction to write a *normative*, one can almost say *canonical*, book [is] unmistakably stamped on his gospel." Cf. H. Strathmann, *Das Evangelium nach Johannes* (NTD, 1954), 5.

96. Schrenk (*TDNT* 1.745) writes, "John . . . in 20:31, when speaking of the aim of his own writing, i.e., to awaken faith . . . can use a word that elsewhere he reserves for OT Scripture, namely, *gegraptai*." Cf. Windisch, *Synoptiker*, 149.

97. See p. 15.

98. Here some understand "prophetic writings" to mean the New Testament inscripturation of the gospel (see, for example, M. J. Lagrange, *Saint Paul Epitre aux Romains* [1931], 379). The New Testament writings, then, would already be characterized by Paul himself as revelatory media in the same way as the Old Testament. Most exegetes, however, including Lagrange, reject this point of view. In any case it appears from a comparison of Rom. 16:26 with passages like Eph. 3:4ff.; Col. 1:25ff.; and 2 Tim. 1:9ff. how much the apostolic activity, whether in word or writing, is presented as the direct and connecting continuation of the Old Testament writings.

99. Also, Ephesians 2:20 mentions the "apostles and prophets." According to some, this can be understood to refer to the Old Testament prophets (see, for example, Arndt and Gingrich, *Greek English Lexicon* [1952], 731, with an appeal to Polycarp, Phil, 6,3), a view that strengthens our argument, but such an interpretation is by no means certain. See, for example, E. Percy, *Die Probleme der Kolosser- und Epheserbrief* (1946), 329; M. Dibelius, *An die Kolosser Epheser*, 3d ed. (1953), 72ff.

100. Namely, in 2 Peter 3:16 where, in our opinion, "the other scriptures" should also be understood to refer to the Old Testament writings. Thus also Schrenk (*TDNT* 1.757) and Fr. Hauck (*Die Kirchenbriefe* [NTD], 101). H. Windisch (*Die Katholischen Briefe* [1930], 105) writes, "By *logoi graphai* are meant the writings of the Old Testament, as well as other early Christian writings, gospels and parenetic writings, which already possessed a kind of canonical esteem both among the heretics and also in the churches." S. Greijdanus is also inclined to this view, *De brieven van de apostelen Petrus en Johannes enz.* (1929), 353.

101. Cf. Schrenk, *TDNT* 1.757.

102. Cf. Kuyper, *Principles*, 467ff.

103. For this point of view, see, for example, Kümmel, "Notwendigkeit," 294–97; H. Berkhof, "De Apostoliciteit der Kerk," in *NedTT* 2 (1947–48): 157ff.; Cullmann, *Tradition*, 28ff.; Skydsgaard, "Christus," 86ff.; and *De apostolische kerk* (1954), 81.

104. See above, pp. 22ff.

105. Cullmann, *Tradition*, 44.

106. See below, pp. 33ff.

107. A. Harnack, *Die Entstehung des neuen Testaments* (1914), 25.

108. See Kümmel ("Notwendigkeit," 300–301), "The necessity that the canon must be closed in principle can only be appreciated and affirmed where the once-for-all, historical character of God's saving activity is not called into question by equating the later church with the apostolic witness. This insight does not make Christianity into a book religion; on the contrary it takes seriously the unrepeatability and the foundational character of earliest Christian history."

109. *Algemeene Canoniek*, 71.

110. Zahn, *Bedeutung*, 36ff.

111. Ibid., 49.

112. Käsemann, "Kanon."

113. Bultmann (*Das Ev. des John, loc. cit.*) also recognizes this.

114. See above, pp. 6–7.

115. For the meaning of this statement in connection with the topic of the apostolicity of the church, see the detailed discussion in *De apostolische kerk* [1954], 52ff.

116. See below, pp. 41ff.

117. See, for example, Grosheide, *Canoniek*, 25.

118. On this question, see *De apostolische kerk*, 43ff., and the literature cited.

119. In this sense, for example, Strathmann (*Das Evangelium nach Johannes* [NTD, 1954, 21] writes that in view of everything in favor of John's authorship of the fourth Gospel, "One [must] really be surprised that critical *doubt about the apostolic origin* of the Fourth Gospel is maintained tenaciously down to the present." The cause of this, according to Strathmann, is to be sought in the fact that the content of the Gospel is regarded to be too supernatural to come from an eyewitness. What settles the matter is "the dogmatic judgment or prejudice that the figure of Christ portrayed in John's Gospel is so far removed from any possible reality that an eyewitness could never have effected the translation of the one into the other, the leap from the one to the other" (21–22). Likewise, Riesenfeld ("Tradition und Redaktion in Markusevangelium," in *Neutest. Studien für Bultmann* [1954], 157) also writes with respect to the problem of the Synoptic tradition, "On the other hand, it is undeniable, however, that the attempted solutions, offered in great number and from the most different sides, are, all together, ultimately and in whatever way conditioned by the position of the respective scholar on the question of the essence of the person of Jesus."

120. "Paul, an apostle, not from men nor through man, but through Jesus Christ, to the brothers who are in Laodicia, grace . . . ." Cf. Gal. 1:1.

121. See already Calvin's judgment, above, p. 10.

122. Cf. G. C. Berkouwer, *De strijd om het Roomsch-Katholieke Dogma*, 101ff.; cf. also G. E. Meuleman, *De ontwikkeling van het dogma in de Rooms-Katholieke Theologie* (1951), 135ff.

123. For the significance of the authority of the church for the recognition of the canon, see Kuyper, *Encyclopaedie* 2.508ff. He distinguishes, however, expressly between the *auctoritas imperii ecclesiae*, which Rome ascribes to the statements of the church as institute, and the *auctoritas dignitatis ecclesiae*, by which he thinks of the church "as an impressive phenomenon in life, with its moral dignity, and which as a creation of Christ bears witness to the *auctor ecclesiae*."

124. See further *De apostolische kerk* (1954), 65ff., and the literature cited.

125. Thus, B. de Moor, *Comment Perp.* (1761), 1.265, quoted by Grosheide, *Canoniek*, 134.

126. The so-called *actio Dei circa Canonem.*

127. See, for example, Kuyper, *Encyclopaedie*, 2.500ff.; 3.40; A. D. R. Polman, *Geloofsbelijdenis*, 1.211ff.

128. Kuyper denies this expressly (*Encycl.*, 3.412), "It must be clearly stated here that the collection of the canon is not included under inspiration. In itself it is natural to think that inspiration was directly involved here. This is, however, not so, and that it is not so may not be disguised." Elsewhere (*Principles*, 546), however, he writes that "ecclesiastical parlance does not permit the conception of inspiration to be entirely ignored in the compiling and editing of the books of the Holy Scripture. This is the less necessary, since in this compiling and editing an activity from the side of God was exerted upon the spirit of man, which, to some extent, is of one kind with real inspiration."

129. Thus, for example, Th. C. Vriezen, "Schriftkritiek en Schriftgezag," *Schrift en Kerk*, 24.

130. See, for example, Grosheide, *Canoniek*, 134.

131. See, for example, A. D. R. Polman, *Geloofsbelijdenis*, 1.212–13.

132. See above, pp. 9–10.

133. See above, p. 10.

134. See above, pp. 6ff.

135. See above, pp. 15ff., 32. And see E. Flesseman-Van Leer, *Tradition and Scripture in the Early Church* (1953), 66–67.

136. For example, the Letter of Barnabas (4:14) and 2 Clement (2:4), where the words of Jesus are introduced with the formulae, "it is written" and "the Scripture says."

137. For proof see, for example, Grosheide, *Canoniek*, 77ff.

138. See, for example, Zahn, *Grundriss der Geschichte des neutest. Kanons* (1904), 39.

139. See Flesseman-Van Leer (*Tradition*, 191), "They deny most decidedly the existence of extrascriptural tradition. To appeal to revelatory truth apart from Scripture is heretical gnosticism."

140. Especially in his *Die Entstehung des neuen Testaments* (1914), 40ff.

141. Thus, J. Knox, *Marcion and the New Testament* (1942).

142. This appears anew from the use that the "Gospel of Truth" (Jung codex), discovered at Nag-Hammadi, makes of most books of the New Testament, as W. C. van Unnik has shown in a careful study. His conclusion is, "Round about 140–150 a collection of writings was known at Rome and accepted as authoritative which was virtually identical with our New Testament" ("The 'Gospel of Truth' and the New Testament," *The Jung Codex* [1955], 124).

143. One may recall the well-known questions that Harnack formulated (*Die Entstehung des N.T.* [1914], 3) and which in part are repeated and expanded by Bultmann (*Theology*, 2.141).

144. *Adv. Haer.*, 3.11.8.

145. Cf. H. Lietzmann, *Wie wurden die Bücher des N.T. heilige Schrift?* (1907), 59.

146. See below, pp. 59–60.

147. See above, p. 26.

148. See the various "Introductions" and "histories of the canon."

149. J. de Zwaan, *Inleiding tot het Nieuwe Testament* (1942), 3.x.

150. Cf. Lietzmann, *Bücher*, 94ff.

151. van Unnik, *The Jung Codex*, 27.

152. Whether the same thing holds with respect to James, which did not belong to "the canon" for a long time, cannot be known with certainty. It was probably cited by Irenaeus (ca. 180). After that, it does not appear in the writings we have. Too little is known about the fortunes of this letter and the causes of its late "canonicity" to reach definite conclusions here.

153. With respect to others, this appeared impossible. Thus the rejection of the Gospel of John by the so-called *alogoi* (also for anti-Montanist motives) did not have any influence in the church.

154. See, for example, Lietzmann, *Bücher*, 91ff.

CHAPTER II

1. Cf. Dinkler, "Bibelautorität," 87.

2. Cf. J. Ridderbos, *Gereformeerde Schriftbeschouwing en organische opvatting* (1926).

3. To these three descriptions of the content of the New Testament, still others can be added. Reference ought to be made especially to *prophecy*, since John 16:13 makes clear that it belongs to the heart of apostolic preaching. We find it alike in the Gospels (especially in the so-called Little Apocalypse of the synoptic Gospels, Mark 13 and parallels), in the Epistles (1 Thess. 4; 2 Thess. 2; 1 Cor. 15; 2 Peter 3; etc.), and especially in Revelation. We shall not treat this otherwise very important concept above, because it would require a hermeneutic treatment that exceeds the proportions of this book.

4. Thus, Friedrich, *TDNT* 3.715ff. Also see H. W. Bartsch, "Kerygma-Theologie?" *EvT* (June, 1952): 572.

5. See especially J. Schniewind, *Euangelion* (1927), 1.34–51; see my *The Coming of the Kingdom* (ET, 1962), 71ff.

6. Friedrich, *TDNT* 3.711ff.; cf. Friedrich, *TDNT* 2.715, n. 90.

7. See below, pp. 68ff.

8. Even if one does not emphasize *ērxato* in Acts 1:1, it should be recognized with Bauernfeind (*Die Apostelgeschichte* [1939], 19) that "this, however, is certain: our author consciously effects the bold and by no means self-evident union of the Jesus-narrative and the missions-narrative as *prōtos logos* and *deuteros logos* of the same work. The course of the gospel over the world is not one of many religious waves arising by chance; rather its power arises solely from the work that Jesus himself accomplished in fulfillment of the ancient promises."

9. Cf. F. W. Grosheide, "The Pauline Epistles as Kerugma," in *Studia Paulina* (in honorem J. de Zwaan, 1953), 139ff.

10. Cf. A. Schweitzer, *The Quest of the Historical Jesus* (ET, 1910).

11. *The So-Called Historical Jesus and the Historic Biblical Christ* (ET, 1964).

12. See my *Zelfopenbaring en Zelfverberging* (1946), 28ff.

13. See Dinkler, "Bibelautorität"; Bartsch, "Kerygma-Theologie?" 571ff. Both are very close to Bultmann.

14. Cf. Bartsch, "Kerygma-Theologie?"

15. See G. C. Berkouwer, *Het probleem der schriftcritiek*, 74ff.; cf. Bartsch, "Kerygma-Theologie?"

16. K. Barth, *Rudolf Bultman, Ein Versuch ihn zu verstehen* (1953).

17. Bartsch, "Kerygma-Theologie?"

18. Berkouwer, *Probleem.*

19. Seek my *The Coming of the Kingdom*, 18ff.

20. In my opinion, it remains to the great credit of such authors as H. Bavinck (*Dogmatiek*, 3.389ff.) and A. Kuyper (*Encycl.*, 3.158–63) that in a time when the concept of the Gospels as "lives of Jesus" was in vogue in exegetical literature, they continued to place all the emphasis on this kerygmatic character, though with other words and in another manner than Kähler.

21. See, for example, K. H. Rengstorf (*Die Auferstehung Jesu* [1954], 10ff.) and N. A. Dahl ("Die Theologie des Neuen Testaments" [a review of Bultmann's work by the same name] in *TR* N.F. [1954], 42), "The decisive question here is this, whether the kerygma, if it is said to be understood as address, cannot at the same time be both a report of the facts and a communication of understanding. Bultmann sees here an exclusive antithesis. But this is not Pauline. Rather, it is the opinion of the apostle that the kerygma is a call to faith just because

it reports an event that has already occurred, both before any decision of the hearer as well as before every proclamation of it, and yet, as God's eschatological act, is simply decisive for the existence of man."

22. See my study "Bultmann," in *The New International Library of Philosophy and Theology*.

23. This must be maintained in opposition to the actualization of the New Testament concept of kerygma by Friedrich (*TDNT* 3.704), "Emphasis does not attach to the *kērygma* as though Christianity contained something decisively new in content. . . . The decisive thing is the action, the proclamation itself. For it accomplishes that which was expected by the OT prophets. The divine intervention takes place through the proclamation. Hence the proclamation itself is the new thing." See 708, "The impartation of the word of the NT must become an act of God. This takes place when He speaks." All this is expressed in a very one-sided manner, to say the least. See 710, "the act of proclamation . . . has this significance, namely, that what is proclaimed is actualized," although Friedrich adds that the content of proclamation is "fixed in advance."

24. See, for example, Jasper's critique of Bultmann in Karl Jaspers and Rudolf Bultmann, *Die Frage der Entmythologisierung* (1954), 41ff., and the demand, put to Bultmann by Buri, for "Entkerygmatisierung," in *Kerygma und Mythos* (1952), 2.85ff.; cf. F. Buri, "Das Selbstverständnis des Christlichens Glaubens als Prinzip der Dogmatik," in *TZ* (1954): 355ff.

25. R. Schippers, *Getuigen van Jezus Christus in het Nieuwe Testament* (1938), 198.

26. Besides Schipper's book (note 25), see especially the very thorough and elaborate article of Strathmann, *TDNT* 4.474ff.

27. *Marturia; marturion* has a somewhat different meaning, cf. Strathmann, *TDNT* 4.502ff.

28. See Strathmann (*TDNT* 4.492), "At issue are, not doctrines, myths, or speculations, but facts which took place in the clear light of history at a specific time and place, facts which can be established and on which we can rely."

29. Strathmann's remark (*TDNT* 4.493) that Acts 22:14ff. and 26:16 are Luke's artificial and unsuccessful attempts to apply the concept of an eyewitness to Paul, therefore, seems inappropriate.

30. See, for example, E. G. Selwyn, *The First Epistle of St. Peter* (1947), 228. According to Windisch (*Die Katholischen Briefe* [1930], 79; cf. S. Greijdanus, *De brieven van de apostelen Petrus en Johannes, en de brief van Judas* [1929], 181), here "personal involvement in these sufferings [is] included."

31. Strathmann, *TDNT* 4.496, n. 63.

32. Thus, Bauernfeind, *Apostelgeschichte*, 7.

33. *Kerygma und Mythos*, 1.48–49.

34. *Theology*, 305.

35. A. J. Rasker, *Het Gezag van de Heilige Schrift* (1954), 13. In opposition to this, Berkhof's remarks in *In the Waagschaal* (Feb. 19, 1954), 2, seem valid: "In orthodox circles that recognize the legitimacy of biblical criticism, one can encounter the view that the deeds of God are authoritative, but that the Bible is the human deposit, record, and witness to them . . . God's deeds are then spoken of in glowing terms, as if here every human role was excluded. And inscripturation is spoken of, then, as a purely human matter. The divine and the human are not to be separated in such a manner."

36. Rasker, *Heilige Schrift*, 10.

37. This also explains the unusual way in which Rasker speaks of "Holy Scripture" and "God's Word." He believes that "we do well to retain these expressions," but that at the same time, there is "everything to be said in favor of sometimes replacing 'obedience to Holy Scripture' by the expression 'obedience to the witness of Holy Scripture.' " The one expression could then guard against individualistic, the other against fundamentalistic, errors (14). All this caution and care to retain the correct (middle-orthodox) standpoint rests, however, on an inner ambiguity. Is the Bible God's Word? If it *is*, then even to oppose Fundamentalism

does not give us the right to "replace this expression" (!) with others that apparently would to some degree deny it. And if it is *not* God's Word, we have no right to call it such, even out of fear of individualism. In my opinion, Rasker's basic error is that he understands the redemptive-historical character of the New Testament witness solely in terms of the content of the witness and not of this witness itself. For that reason, it makes no sense to replace the expression "obedience to the Holy Scripture" with the expression "obedience to the witness of Holy Scripture." The Scripture is holy just because it has this witness-character.

38. G. C. van Niftrik, *Woord en Dienst* (June 19, 1954), 203.

39. H. Berkhof (*In de Waagschaal* [March 5, 1954], 176) writes with respect to the historical investigation of the Bible, "It is here evident, if anywhere, that neutral critical investigation, although theoretically conceivable, is practically unworkable." But later he adds, "Yet we do not plead for a 'Christian-scientific investigation of the Bible.' In the field of science, every scholar has a right to speak, provided he knows where science ends and ideology begins." But is it possible to distinguish this "where" in the study of Scripture, unless at the same time one discerns the nature of Scripture by faith? And is there any possibility for an *adequate* scientific investigation other than by doing it in a "Christian" way, in the sense of a "believing" manner?

40. Cf. Strathmann, *TDNT* 4.492.

41. See above, p. 59.

42. See above, pp. 63–64.

43. Cf. G. C. Berkouwer, *The Triumph of Grace in the Theology of Karl Barth* (1956), 276ff.

44. Cf. K. Goldammer, "Die Frage der Entmythologisierung im Lichte der Religionsgeschichte," in *TLZ* (1953): 755.

45. See, for example, S. H. Spanjaard, *De Christusverkondiging aan de buitenkerkelijke mens* (1954), 100ff.

46. Nils A. Dahl, "Anamnesis. Mémoire et Commémoration dans le christianisme primitif," *ST* 1 (1948): 80. He adds (in my judgment, correctly), "Therefore what we generally understand by 'preaching,' the sermon as it currently takes place in church, does not simply correspond to the New Testament *kērussein*, but rather, in many respects, to *hupomimnēskein* 'to recall to mind'," cf. C. H. Dodd, *The Apostolic Preaching*, 9.

47. See above, note 3.

48. In his article in *TDNT* 2.140, 144ff. See, in contrast, Cremer-Kögel, *Bibl. Theol. Wörterbuch des neutest. Griechisch* (11th ed., 1923), 292ff.

49. Therefore it is also very one-sided when Rengstorf (*TDNT* 2.141) writes that what is new in the word usage of the Gospels is "the complete supersession of the intellectual element present in the non-biblical usage."

50. See J. Schniewind (*Das Evangelium nach Matthaus* [1937], 35): "The contrast is not material in character."

51. Cremer-Kögel (*Wörterbuch*, 292) makes a distinction by saying that "*kērussein*, to which *akouein* corresponds, designates . . . bare communication, respectively, the summons attaching to it, while *didaskein*, in contrast, to which *manthanein* corresponds, designates instruction, teaching activity aimed at effecting the understanding and which substantiates, elucidates, and enters into the subject matter in detail."

52. Cf. Cremer-Kögel, *Wörterbuch*, 293.

53. See, for example, the extensive elaborations of Bultmann on "The Development of Doctrine" in *Theology*, 2.119–42; see 1.65.

54. See my *Paul and Jesus*, 56ff.

55. Cf. Bultmann, *TDNT* 1.708.

56. From this point of view, it is necessary (in my opinion) to exercise criticism on the "concept of truth," as Berkhof describes this in his writing, *Gods Ene kerk en onze vele kerken* (n.d.), 50–51.

57. See Greijdanus (*Het heilig Evangelie naar de beschrijving van Lucas* [1940], 1.549) on Luke 11:24.

58. "Elemental spirits" or "world spirits." But see the contrary view of this expression in my *The Epistle of Paul to the Churches of Galatia* (1953), 153ff.

59. See what Bultmann ("The Problem of Hermeneutics," *Essays Philosophical and Theological* [ET, 1955], 252ff.) calls the "preunderstanding" for the interpretation of the New Testament.

60. Cf. Bavinck, *Dogmatiek*, 1.450f.

61. *Nouthetein.*

62. *Parakalein.*

INDEX OF SCRIPTURE

90